Antagonism on YouTube

Also Available From Bloomsbury

Antagonism on YouTube

Metaphor in Online Discourse

Stephen Pihlaja

B L O O M S B U R Y

LONDON • NEW DELHI • NEW YORK • SYDNEY

Bloomsbury Academic
An imprint of Bloomsbury Publishing Plc

50 Bedford Square	1385 Broadway
London	New York
WC1B 3DP	NY 10018
UK	USA

www.bloomsbury.com

Bloomsbury is a registered trade mark of Bloomsbury Publishing Plc

First published 2014

British Library Cataloguing-in-Publication Data
A catalogue record for this book is available from the British Library.

ISBN: HB: 978-1-4725-6667-6
ePDF: 978-1-4725-6669-0
ePub: 978-1-4725-6668-3

Library of Congress Cataloging-in-Publication Data
Pihlaja, Stephen.
Antagonism on Youtube: metaphor in online discourse / Stephen Pihlaja.
pages cm
Includes bibliographical references and index.
ISBN 978-1-4725-6667-6 (hardback) — ISBN 978-1-4725-6668-3 (epub) —
ISBN 978-1-4725-6669-0 (epdf) 1. Christianity–Computer network resources. 2. YouTube
(Electronic resource) 3. Metaphor–Religious aspects–Christianity. 4. Interpersonal
conflict–Religious aspects–Christianity. 5. Discourse analysis–Religious
aspects–Christianity. I. Title.
BR99.74P54 2014
303.602856754–dc23
2014006139

Typeset by RefineCatch Limited, Bungay, Suffolk
Printed and bound in Great Britain

Contents

1

Drama in the YouTube Community

The YouTube community is diverse. On any given day, YouTube's most-viewed list is populated by a hotchpotch of internet miscellanea: the home videos of a self-proclaimed bearded internet clown and his family, a pop artist's newest controversial music video, a German TV presenter unable to control embarrassing laughter, or an attractive young woman staring silently and longingly at a camera. YouTube has afforded internet wealth and fame to the notorious video camera-toting uncle at the last family gathering while allowing political dissidents suffering under repressive regimes to make their plight known to the world.

This book focuses on the YouTube world somewhere in between videos of cats playing pianos and Presidential speeches – the small but passionate community of individuals discussing religious issues on the site. In a utopian vision of the internet, the affordance of instant access to the lives and faces of users from different backgrounds, faith traditions, and geopolitical perspectives allows the free exchange of ideas and philosophy, with users considering one another's opinions, building on those ideas, and moving towards greater understanding. In reality, however, YouTube interaction is far more antagonistic and YouTube comments threads are notorious for vicious and mean-spirited exchanges.

YouTube provides both a service for users to upload and publish digital video online, and a 'web 2.0' environment where users not only consume content, but interact socially with others. YouTube's interactive features provide many opportunities for user text production and interaction, including usernames linked to YouTube channels; video-hosting; text attached to videos including titles, video descriptions, and 'tags' (keywords); and comments on videos. Users can upload videos of themselves speaking to the camera (called 'vlogs') about any topic or issue that interests them. Others can then make text comments on the video or record their own videos in response, creating a video or comment 'thread' in which videos and responses follow a common topic of interaction over an extended period.

YouTube pages are complex sites of interaction, with different elements (such as comments, description boxes, keyword 'tags', and the video) contained on the page, all with different features of text production. Beyond basic community standards forbidding violent and pornographic videos, YouTube does not restrict what types of video can be posted on the site, and different users produce different content, from corporate channels hosting music videos, television shows and commercials, to individual users producing comedy skits, family videos, vlogs, and so on. As the videos in my dataset are 'vlogs', a brief history of the genre is needed before considering how it might best be analysed.

The neologism 'vlog' is a portmanteau comprised of the words 'video' and 'blog'. Vlogging as a practice emerged in 2006 with YouTube's rising popularity and the combined technical advancements of abundant, free online video storage space and inexpensive web cameras (Burgess & Green, 2009). The generic conventions of the vlog, however, have grown out of an older computer-mediated communication (CMC) genre, the 'blog', which began to gain popularity in the early 2000s as a new kind of personal webpage in which users could post reverse chronological updates about topics of their choosing (Blood, 2004). Although the exact parameters of what a blog is or is not have been hotly contested, Herring and colleagues (Herring et al., 2004:11) see a distinction between 'journal-style' blogs, which are similar to online journals, and 'filter-style' blogs, which provide information about different topics for a particular community, with intermediate characteristics, such as allowing a user to express themselves with varying degrees of exposure in an online space they can control.

The influence of the journal-style, confessional blog can be seen in the vlog's generic conventions. Users make videos alone, directly addressing a camera as though talking to another person, paradoxically engaging no one and everyone at the same time. Although, as with blogs, the bounds of what is and is not a vlog are not always clear, Burgess and Green have suggested the very simple description of a vlog video as 'a talking head, a camera, and some editing' (Burgess & Green, 2008:6), to which I add, drawing on Herring's description of blogs as online journals, 'with a sense of free expression of one's own opinions and experiences in an online, public space'. What is or is not a 'vlog' is not simply defined and the term has continued to develop with a diversity of uses on YouTube, but the vlogs in my dataset are all non-professionally produced videos with, in most cases, users speaking directly to the camera with little or no post-production editing.

As on many internet sites, interaction on YouTube often features confrontational, antagonistic exchanges among users, and YouTube comments in particular are known for their offensive content. The term 'drama' (or 'flame wars' as it has been known in other internet genres) appears often as an emic label for a phenomenon 'that emerge[s] when a flurry of video posts clusters around an internal "controversy" and/or antagonistic debate between one or more YouTubers' (Burgess & Green, 2008:13). In these cases, serious disagreements can become entangled with interpersonal relationships and users position themselves in relation to others and social controversies.

'Drama' plays a key role in YouTube interaction by giving users subject matter for videos, affording them with creative ways to insult one another, and providing a chance for users to support or oppose others. Drama videos are often made quickly in response to other users with little production or planning and are also often removed within days or even hours of being posted. Although the actual video pages (i.e. videos and comments) may not remain, the talk that ensues in their absence, particularly the reconstruction of what another user may or may not have said, remains in response videos, both in references to the video by the user who removed it, and in reporting of 'what someone said' on separate video pages. This leads to a complex, dynamic network of new, old, and missing video pages, with drama developing from previous disagreements, the reconstruction of previous videos and comments, and user reassessment and repositioning as the context changes.

Internet drama is, of course, nothing new. Antagonism on the internet has long been of interest to researchers from the disciplines of sociology, psychology, anthropology, religious studies, and linguistics, including, for example, early work on lack of co-operation in Usenet groups (Kollock & Smith, 1996), antagonism in controlled experimental environments (Dubrovsky, Kiesler, & Sethna, 1991), and politeness strategies in e-mail discussion groups (Harrison, 2000). In early analysis of online interaction, researchers focused on the effects of anonymity in CMC. Hardaker (citing

Kiesler, Siegel, & McGuire, 1984; Siegel, Dubrovsky, Kiesler, & McGuire, 1986) states that 'CMC can offer a very high degree of anonymity, and a great deal more control over a self-presentation than is available face-to-face (FtF), but this anonymity can also foster a sense of impunity, loss of self-awareness, and a likelihood of acting upon normally inhibited impulses, an effect known as deindividuation' (Hardaker, 2010:224). Although social media sites like Facebook and YouTube offer less anonymity than earlier, primarily text-based technologies, an effect of deindividuation created by communicating through internet technology seems to persist.

YouTube has been of particular interest for research into 'flaming' (or negative messages sent on the internet) given its reputation for negative interaction (Burgess & Green, 2008; Lange, 2007a). Recent studies, including analyses of user experience (Lange, 2007b), user perceptions of 'flaming' in comments (Moor, Heuvelman, & Verleur, 2010), responses to the anti-Islam film 'Fitna' (van Zoonen, Vis, & Mihelj, 2011; Vis, van Zoonen, & Mihelj, 2011), and impoliteness strategies in responses to the 'Obama Reggaeton' video (Lorenzo-Dus, Garcés-Conejos Blitvich, & Bou-Franch, 2011), have investigated 'antagonism' in user responses to particular videos and topics.

From these studies of YouTube 'antagonism' and 'flaming', several important gaps remain in descriptions of antagonism on YouTube and of YouTube drama in particular. First, although Burgess and Green's (2009) description of 'drama' provides a basic outline for the phenomenon, no research has been done looking at a particular occurrence of YouTube drama and no empirical description of YouTube drama based on systematic analysis of YouTube video pages has yet been produced. Second, research into YouTube 'flaming' and 'antagonism' has focused on text comments and user reports, but analysis of the interaction between discourse in the video and text comments in a particular YouTube community context has not been done. Video pages, particularly those made by vloggers, are situated in a particular social context, and understanding the history of interaction between users is important for a full analysis. Third, close discourse analysis of video talk remains rare. Historically, analysis of YouTube interaction has focused on comments, given the ease of collecting the data, but insomuch as video talk represents the main content of the video page, analysis of video talk is essential for describing and analysing responses in comments and subsequent videos.

The study of 'flaming' and online antagonism, however, sits in a much larger discussion of how and why people are 'impolite' with one another. The study of impoliteness has developed in the last twenty years in tandem with the development of theories of politeness in language (Bousfield & Locher, 2008). Perhaps most influentially, Brown and Levinson's (1987) 'face-saving' politeness theory has had a substantial influence on how individual acts of impoliteness have been analysed, particularly in terms of the 'intentional' impoliteness of 'flaming' in online interaction. Brown and Levinson's theory is built on the notion that speakers attempt to save 'positive face', or the positive value they claim for themselves. 'Face' as an analytic principle was originally defined by the sociologist Goffman as 'the positive social value a person effectively claims for himself [sic] by the line others assume he has taken during a particular contact' (Goffman, 1967:5), but Brown and Levinson further distinguished between *negative face*, or 'the want of every "competent adult member" that his actions are unimpeded by others' and *positive face*, or 'the want of every member that his wants be desirable to at least some others' (Brown & Levinson, 1987:62). Brown and Levinson also developed the concept of a 'face-threatening act' (FTA) (i.e. an action that might undermine the face considerations of a hearer in an interaction) and propose a series of possible actions a person may take in relation to realizing a FTA (Brown & Levinson, 1987:60). Brown and Levinson then rank the choices that a speaker might take in terms of politeness depending on the speaker's estimation of how an FTA might affect the hearer's face concerns.

Although O'Driscoll (1996) notes that Brown and Levinson's 'face dualism' has been successfully employed in various cultural contexts including Singapore and Japan (Kuiper & Lin, 1989; Tokunaga, 1992), he also notes early criticism that 'face dualism' is not a universal concept (Gu, 1990; Matsumoto, 1988), that Brown and Levinson's exposition of 'face dualism' in politeness is inaccurate (Ide, 1989; Matsumoto, 1989), and that inapplicable data can be found (Mao, 1994; Nwoye, 1992). Criticism in these instances largely centred on employing Brown and Levinson's understanding of 'face' in non-Western cultures, particularly cultures in which priority is placed on the 'wants' of the group over individual wants.

Given that tracing the discourse comprising YouTube drama requires understanding how users view themselves and their action within the community, the concept of 'face' does serve some purpose in describing how users want and do not want to be perceived. However, as O'Driscoll (1996) and Terkourafi (2008) suggest, the notion of 'face' is certainly not unproblematic, particularly when attempting to draw 'universals' (as Brown and Levinson sought) across cultures. Although a simple, universal notion of 'face' may not be applicable, as both O'Driscoll and Terkourafi also suggest, lack of a universal cultural 'face' does not negate the useful descriptive properties of the term. With care taken to understanding the cultural components of 'face', Brown and Levinson's definitions of 'positive' and 'negative face' serve initially as a useful description of how users desire to be perceived and treated in interaction.

Additionally, the Brown and Levinson model of face-threatening acts may not adequately take into account the dynamic nature of interaction because it focuses on speaker intent and cognition (problematic in their own right), but not on the hearer (Werkhofer, 1992). In Brown and Levinson's model, face-threatening acts may prove an insufficiently dynamic conception of interaction, one in which speakers act and respond in strategic ways with individual acts that can then be isolated and analysed. In addition to a need for a nuanced understanding of 'face' and FTAs in dynamic discourse, Locher (2004) points out that Brown and Levinson's definition of politeness essentially values indirectness as the 'ultimate realisation' of politeness, but that impoliteness can also be indirect. In describing the discourse dynamics of YouTube drama, rather than seeing impoliteness as a single purposeful act, it may be more useful to see how words and/or actions are evaluated as such and how different users respond to the words and/or actions of others that they view negatively.

The influence of Brown and Levinson's 'face-threatening acts' on the development of definitions of 'impoliteness' can be seen throughout the history of impoliteness research, starting with Culpeper's description of 'impoliteness' as 'the use of strategies designed to attack face, and thereby cause social conflict or disharmony' (Culpeper, Bousfield, & Wichmann, 2003:1545). Culpeper subsequently refined the definition to take into account both speakers and hearers, stating that, 'Impoliteness comes about when: (1) the speaker communicates face-attack intentionally, or (2) the hearer perceives and/or constructs behaviour as intentionally face-attacking, or a combination of (1) and (2)' (Culpeper, 2005:38). Bousfield (2008) further shifts Culpeper and colleagues' definition by suggesting that impoliteness can be viewed as intentional or unintentional, depending both on the speaker's reported intent and on the meaning that the hearer constructs from the speaker's words. These definitions remain problematic because intentionality remains difficult to recover, especially as the analyst must rely on reports of intention in the data. Culpeper subsequently (Culpeper, 2008, 2011) downplays the importance of identifying intent in impolite interaction, relying on Gibbs' description of intention as the 'dynamic, emergent properties of interactive social/cultural/ historical moments within which people create and make sense of different human artefacts' (Gibbs, 1999:17). In this sense, 'intention' is not a static object for the analyst or the hearer to recover, but something dependent on and changing with speaker reports of their intention and perception of speaker intent. Culpeper's (2011) most recent description of impoliteness does not include intent, stating instead that:

> Impoliteness is a negative attitude towards specific behaviours occurring in specific contexts. It is sustained by expectations, desires and/or beliefs about social organization, including, in particular, how one person's or a group's identities are mediated by others in interaction. Situated behaviours are viewed negatively – considered 'impolite' – when they conflict with how one expects them to be, how one wants them to be and/or how one thinks they ought to be.
>
> (Culpeper, 2011:23)

In this revised description, Culpeper focuses on perception of specific behaviours (i.e. words and actions) in specific social contexts rather than the intent of the speaker. Employing this description then requires considering how the actions of an individual are perceived by others in the same social organization or community, and to what extent they do or do not conform to expectations. Culpeper (2008) sees four different kinds of norms interacting in different contexts to influence a person's expectations about impoliteness:

- 'Personal norms' based on the totality of an individual's social experiences.
- 'Cultural norms' based on the totality of an individual's experiences of a particular culture.
- 'Situational norms' based on the totality of an individual's experiences of a particular situation in a particular culture.
- 'Co-textual norms' based on the totality of an individual's experience of a particular interaction in a particular situation in a particular culture.

(Culpeper, 2008:30)

What is or is not considered impolite can therefore differ greatly depending on the norms an individual expects at any given time in any given situation. As expectations, desires and beliefs about social organization differ among contexts, what is and is not perceived as impoliteness will differ depending on speakers, hearers, and observers. Particularly within a YouTube community, for example, expectations about how others should behave, and what is and is not appropriate, are fluid depending on the particular users interacting on particular video pages and what each individual user expects of the others. The shared repertoire of negotiable resources of a particular community may also lead to changing 'situational' and 'cultural' norms.

In analysis of impoliteness, Locher (2004) suggests that struggles for power need always to be a fundamental analytic consideration, and the link between impoliteness and power has also been of continuous interest to researchers. Building on Kasper's (1990) notion of 'motivated' rudeness, Beebe (1995) identifies three purposes that 'instrumental rudeness' serves: to appear superior, to get power over actions, and to get power in conversation. In all these instances, the speaker moves to impose him- or herself as the dominant actor in a social situation and take up a position of power. What constitutes a position of power, however, might be unclear particularly considering different conceptions of power that other users might hold.

On YouTube, the role of impoliteness in dominance is of particular importance because, although Burgess and Green (2009) describe 'drama' in terms of 'antagonistic debate', YouTube users often also describe interaction on the site in terms of 'p'wning' or 'p'wnage' (i.e. dominating another user completely, as in an online game) (Pfannenstiel, 2010). In instances of p'wnage, dominance of another user is an explicit goal of the interaction, with users trying to display their ability to argue their position so convincingly that the other cannot respond, similar to Michael Billig's (1996) notion of the 'last word' in which opponents continue to answer the claims of the other in an attempt to leave the other speechless. How impoliteness operates in dominance over other users, however, remains an open and important question for understanding how drama develops. It requires an awareness of the institutional factors present in interaction within a YouTube community since the interaction among users is always situated in a larger socio-historical context.

A close description of dynamic contextual factors and the outcome of impoliteness, therefore, must be taken into account to understand how and why antagonism develops in particular communities. The studies of YouTube interaction I have so far mentioned, however, reflect the trends of prior CMC research, employing interviews, questionnaires, discourse analysis, and ethnography to describe the YouTube community in more general terms and attempts to adapt research methods for YouTube have been incomplete in taking into account all elements of the video page as well as the dynamic nature of interactions on the site. With very little discourse analysis of full video pages, research into YouTube discourse has continued to rely on analysis of comments and user reports of experience. This study, therefore, addresses a gap that remains in close discourse analysis of talk from YouTube video pages in the interaction of specific users over time.

Although a growing body of research into YouTube social interaction continues to develop descriptions of user experience on YouTube, empirical studies of how YouTube 'drama' develops is rare. Rather than attempt to describe and analyse overall user experience, this book focuses on the interaction of a small group of users discussing issues of Christian theology and atheism on the site, analysing how drama develops over time and how users position themselves and others in relation to changing contexts. Since YouTube drama occurs publicly, the research will focus on actual YouTube video pages rather than user reports of their actions and responses. The aim of this book is, therefore, to investigate how and why YouTube drama develops through a systematic description and analysis of user discourse. Through close analysis of video pages, this study contributes to a greater academic understanding of internet antagonism and YouTube interaction by revealing the factors that contribute to the development of drama over time.

Because YouTube drama is an emergent phenomenon, developing out of the individual interactions on video pages, it often cannot be identified until after it has occurred. Drama can develop between two users in isolated single video threads or in comments sections in which two individuals have a disagreement. However, drama can also occur on a larger scale among groups of affiliated users when individual comments and/or video responses become broader disagreements. Drama also does not often have clear beginnings and endings, with past interactions, friendships, and new disagreements affecting how users interact with one another and how they position themselves either in opposition to or affiliation with others. Accurately describing and analysing YouTube drama, therefore, requires situating individual instances of interaction within broader contexts of the YouTube 'community'.

CMC researchers and internet users have understood and described social interaction online by comparison and contrast to offline social spaces, particularly through descriptions of what have been called online 'communities' (see Journal of Computer Mediated Communication, 2005). In her seminal work on the subject of 'online community', Herring (2004) operationalizes 'community' for computer-mediated discourse analysis. First identifying the origin of the 'virtual community' concept (Rheingold, 1993; 2000) and acknowledging early concerns that the term 'community' may have grown too broad to be useful (Fernback & Thompson, 1995; Jones, 1995), Herring analyses discussion forums from two professional development websites to investigate what constitutes an 'online community'. Based on her analysis, Herring (2004) suggests that an online community can be identified through similarities in structure (such as jargon, ingroup/outgroup language), meaning (exchange of knowledge, negotiation of meaning), interaction (reciprocity, extended [in-depth] threads, core participants), social behaviour (solidarity, conflict management, norms of appropriateness), and participation (frequent, regular, self-sustaining activity over time). Although online communities may differ in the configuration of these features, they are all necessary for the development of an online community.

This notion and treatment of community is, however, partially problematic in describing the interaction of YouTube users in drama. Although participation and interaction can be observed as well as some elements of shared structure in language use (in terms of the generic norms of vlogging in particular), users do not necessarily share social behaviours or ingroup/outgroup language (to use Herring's terms). In the YouTube community, users from diverse backgrounds interact with one another, and there are no functions that allow for users to create formal 'groups' which are moderated. Moreover, because users have different socio-political perspectives and socio-cultural backgrounds without a mutually agreed upon goal for interaction, they do not necessarily have the same expectations.

Community of practice theory takes a markedly different approach to community. Developed out of Lave and Wenger's theorization of social learning (Lave & Wenger, 1991), this view of community focuses how specific shared knowledge emerged in interaction between community members around a shared practice. Although further work by Wenger and colleagues (Wenger et al., 2002) described the development of a community in clear, definable stages, community of practice theory treats community formation as social organization that is explicitly emergent (Wenger, 1998). Cox warns that '[although] a surface reading would see a community of practice as a unified, neatly bounded group ... what is intended is a far more subtle concept' (Cox, 2005), one in which communities are primarily bound by mutual engagement, a joint negotiated enterprise, and a shared repertoire of negotiable resources accumulated over time (Wenger, 1998). Membership in a community, therefore, is defined by what members practise, not whether or not they explicitly identify as community members.

Given the diversity of users on YouTube, the lack of shared identification, and the lack of a gatekeeping mechanism by which members can enter and leave the community, community theory offers a useful, dynamic perspective of how community membership on YouTube might best be understood as activity rather than identity. In this book, I therefore describe YouTube as a site where users form different communities of practice. Each community features:

- shared mutual engagement: communication in videos, comments, private messages, and potentially outside of the site;
- a joint negotiated enterprise: making videos;
- shared repertoire of negotiable resources including:
  - technological materials needed to make the videos, such as a web-camera, internet connection, and computer
  - sustained mutual relationships
  - shared ways of making videos
  - mutually defining identities
  - shared stories and inside jokes
  - knowledge of past interaction in the community
  - knowledge or expertise in topics most often addressed in the community.

On YouTube, the shared repertoire of negotiable resources could differ among the community depending on who engages whom and what topics the community tends to discuss. The shared repertoire of negotiable resources is also dependent on the relationships within an individual community, the history of interaction, and the influence of different members at different times. For example, in the community analysed in this study, the Bible is an important shared resource for some participants. Since community membership depends on engagement, users can enter and leave YouTube at different times, users can have stronger or weaker attachments to the community based on the level of their engagement, and some users can be more prominent on YouTube at different times depending on their own engagement with others and the strength of the shared resources with other users. The boundaries of the community are, thus, fluid and changing as the members, the mutual engagement, and resources change.

As with impoliteness, power is an important consideration in community of practice theory because although community might be conceived as democratic structures given their emergent properties, Roberts (2006) argues that a community member has the ability to dominate others in a community if he or she limits the 'fullness' of another member's participation. Who has and controls knowledge can also lead to unequal relationships. Because communities are built on the creation, transfer, and holding of knowledge, organizational and institutional structures can also exert control over knowledge (Coopey & Burgoyne, 2000) and expert knowledge created outside of the community can be valued over local knowledge (Yanow, 2004). De Latt (2002) found in analysing messages between police officers in an online forum that the content of participation (particularly what sort of information members provide and how it compares to other member contributions) must be considered in addition to the quantity of participation. Who is contributing, when they are contributing, and how others respond is then enormously important to how a community develops and who has power within it.

Considering the work done to date, this book attempts something new. Rather than try to make broad generalization about YouTube antagonism using large corpora of YouTube comments or videos, I analyse an actual incidence of drama in a particular community, and describe and analyse how that drama develops over time. Doing discourse analysis after a period of longitudinal observation (Androutsopoulos, 2008), I will look at one drama 'event', in which an Evangelical Christian user, claiming to be quoting the Bible, called another user 'human garbage'. The community erupted in response and the subsequent drama touched on several key issues: how users can and should interpret the Bible, what a 'Christian' should or should not say in the community, and what roles different members play. To describe and analyse the drama, I will employ a toolkit of discourse analytic methods, starting with an analysis of metaphor and extending this analysis to how users employed categories and positioned one another. The analysis will then show that 'drama', rather than a simple exchange of insults between users, is actually much more complex, revealing beliefs about the social world and what the YouTube community should be.

2

YouTube as a Field: Life in a YouTube Community

Entering the field

The flamboyant, aggressive atheist user capnoawesome initially sparked my interest in religious dialogue on YouTube. capnoawesome's videos and interactions with users were over the top, treating religious users and beliefs with contempt in mocking videos. His aggressive, argumentative personality, however, eventually lead to him closing his account after video of himself and another user having sex was posted online without the other user's permission and the community largely blamed capnoawesome for leaking the video after he boasted about it. Although capnoawesome's presence on the site was ultimately short-lived, his videos allowed me to identify other popular atheist users on YouTube through reading comments and watching video responses, and I built a subscription list of YouTube atheists I found interesting.

In late 2006 and early 2007, atheists on YouTube gained some notoriety when a group called the 'Rational Response Squad', which encouraged users to make videos of themselves 'blaspheming the holy spirit' (a reference to Matthew 12.31) which Jesus warns is the one unforgivable sin. The videos garnered attention on news programmes in the United States, focusing attention on the movement's organizers alleged targeting of minors for the challenge by giving away free DVDs. Although this topic eventually fell out of interest on the site, the issue seemed to expose an apparent growth and popularity of atheism on YouTube, corresponding loosely with the emergence of 'New Atheism' offline and references to Richard Dawkins, Sam Harris, and Daniel Dennett were often heard in atheist user videos.

Around this time in the spring of 2007, I also became aware of Christian users on YouTube for the first time, through the responses of popular atheist users to arguments made against them by Christian users, and I began to subscribe to Christian users as well as atheist users. In 2007, the environment on YouTube was still mostly unregulated and the practice of maliciously 'p'wning' or attacking users was quite prominent. As there was little recourse to censor another's opinion or limit how users spoke about each other, vicious and aggressive personal attacks were common and often lead users to close their accounts to stop the harassment. Although this atmosphere continues to an extent on YouTube, with several means to take action against other users (including filing a digital millennium copyright act (DMCA) complaint against users who infringe on your copyright) and several public cases of popular user accounts being taken down due to complaints, the atmosphere in 2007 was quite different.

One Christian user in my subscription list, jezuzfreek777 (known to everyone as jezuzfreek), frequently engaged in dialogue with atheist users and was ridiculed and quite often mocked on the site. jezuzfreek and TheAmazingAtheist (another prominent, popular YouTube atheist) frequently made videos in response to one another. Near the end of 2007, dialogue threads between Christians and atheist users became of particular interest to me as they seemed to highlight how users were able to ignore the arguments of each other while using the pretence of argumentation and dialogue as an attempt to spread their own message. In December of 2008, I observed the first dialogue that I would formally analyse (Pihlaja, 2010, 2011). In the dialogue, an atheist user, fakesagan, engaged jezuzfreek on the issue of stem cell research, but very quickly the dialogue became about personal issues between the two users and how fakesagan felt that prior behaviour by jezuzfreek was not acceptable, calling him the 'pope of YouTube'. The argument highlighted how personal differences between users far removed from each other both in distance and ideology could lead to disagreements about even basic questions of YouTube politeness. To me, the discussions between the two evidenced the difficulties of not only online communication, but inter-religious and inter-cultural dialogue. I began, in January of 2008, to maintain a more systematic subscription list of 15–20 atheist/ non-religious users and 15–20 Christian users, focusing on identifying moments of disagreement between users and extended antagonistic interaction.

The user Yokeup first came to my attention in May 2007 when he made a video that was widely ridiculed in the atheist community. In the video, he claimed that more US soldiers had died in combat under President Bill Clinton than had died under President George W. Bush, a figure that was highly suspect given the prevalent coverage of soldier deaths in the Iraq War at the time. Yokeup had, it appeared, misread some data and eventually apologized for his mistake, but his brazen assertion of the fact which was clearly false along with his engaging personality and personal narrative made him quite interesting to me as a viewer.

Yokeup became a Christian in 2005. Although he had been a successful business man in the past, he had fallen on hard times several years earlier. He was several times divorced and homeless when he had a 'salvation moment'. After his conversion experience, Yokeup became a trucker and met a woman named Caroline on a Christian dating site. Caroline also had a very compelling testimony: she had been a lesbian who was suicidal and depressed, but had also experienced a Christian conversion that included renouncing her homosexual lifestyle. They married in May 2006 and Yokeup went to work with Caroline at her father's company American Water Treatment (AWT), which delivers salt for water treatment facilities in the New Orleans, Louisiana area in the Southern United States.

Yokeup and Caroline together founded Yokeup Ministries, a non-profit religious organization committed to spreading the gospel both on YouTube and in their local community. Although their videos were often playful and fun, they included a very serious message about the need for salvation and the coming judgement of God. Over the three years I observed them, they used different tropes with differing degrees of regularity, including videos of Yokeup and Caroline driving while sermon audio plays, of preaching at a local truckstop where they 'do church' on Sunday mornings, of delivering salt and meeting and sharing the gospel with people in New Orleans, and many others. Caroline has made several videos denouncing homosexuality as perversion and claiming that there is no such thing. As a Christian she claimed to have been completely reformed from homosexuality by her religious experience. Yokeup and Caroline often both appeared in their work shirts and both were heavily tattooed, embodying working-class personas. They were also politically conservative and have made videos attending right-wing 'tea party' protests in America, demanding small government, fewer taxes, and greater States rights.

At the time I began observing him, Yokeup was friends with many Christian users on YouTube, including jthunder73. jthunder73, who went by his real first name Javid, is a middle-aged black American living in the Chicago area and another member of the YouTube Christian community. Although he referred to himself as 'Pastor Javid' and his name was cited as pastor at a church website in Chicago, his ministry appeared to be primarily a volunteer one. He worked as an insurance salesman for a large US insurance provider and had a large family who featured in many of his videos. In spring 2008, Javid made a video discussing his position on abortion. In the video, Javid told the story of a woman in his congregation who was an undergraduate student at a Chicago university. One day, she was abducted by a group of men, gang raped, and then released. She became pregnant and Javid counselled her to keep the child despite her desire to abort the pregnancy. The child was born, but due to the stress of the event and the resemblance of the child to one of the rapists, the woman killed herself and the child. The video Javid made was quite emotional and ended with him admitting that he felt as though he gave the woman the wrong advice.

After the video was posted, Yokeup began to question the story's authenticity and asked Javid to present some evidence that it was true. Although Yokeup and Javid had been friends prior to the video, their relationship deteriorated as Yokeup aggressively sought out information about the 'Latasha mystery' as he called it. Eventually, Yokeup began to make attack videos directed at Javid, implying at one point that Javid had an adulterous relationship and created this story as a way to cover it up. The initial video that Javid made was subsequently taken down and Javid made several videos explaining why he was not giving the information. He claimed that he had been sued by the family of 'Latasha' and could not release her real name because of the legal dispute and other users posted videos saying that Javid had told them the real name and Yokeup was wrong to continue demanding it. Yokeup on several occasions reuploaded with commentary the original video that Javid had made, but all of the original videos were also subsequently removed and most of Yokeup's commentary on the specific event has been deleted, although attacks on Javid still present on his channel at the end of my observation.

In January of 2008, Yokeup closed his primary channel and began making videos on his yokedtojesus channel as well as on his knuckleheadreview and knuckleheadreality channels. Although no video was ever made explaining the closure of his channel, Yokeup alluded to a sense that the channel had become more about him than the ministry. There was some discussion that he had received a strike (or a notice of warning from YouTube) on his account for reuploading other's content without permission, but these claims could not be verified and would only be known by Yokeup. Javid did not provide any of the information that Yokeup requested and a split in the Christian community could be seen between individuals who thought Javid was lying and those who supported Javid. The support from the atheist/non-religious users seemed to come from users who felt as though Yokeup's behaviour was mean-spirited and inappropriate, and supporting Javid was used, for some, including the atheist user Crosisborg, as a way to attack Yokeup as being unreasonable.

The initial disagreement between Yokeup and Javid also included some underlying issues of theology, race, and politics. First, Javid preached and was a pastor at a primarily black church in Chicago, and the theological and stylistic differences between the urban, Pentecostal approach to Christianity and Yokeup's disposition seemed to aggravate the situation as both viewed Christianity in different ways. Javid also had formal theological training, which he regularly drew on in his exegesis, while Yokeup relied heavily on what he claimed God told him about scripture. Second, in 2008, the Presidential race played an important role in many videos and Javid was a vocal supporter of Barack Obama which Yokeup claimed regularly that one could not be a Christian and vote for Obama and later, that Obama was actually a Muslim pretending to be a Christian.

Although the 'Latasha mystery' as well as the underlying denominational, theological, and racial issues were complex and users seemed to agree or disagree with Yokeup to different degrees at different times, there was a sense in Yokeup's talk around the topic that the more moderate Christians had sided with Javid and that the 'saved' or 'born-again' conservative Christians were siding with him. Those who Yokeup called out as being supporters of Javid and 'ooshy, gooshies' or 'soft' Christians, disagreed at different levels with Yokeup, some refusing to interact with him, some attempting to interact with him in deferential and kind ways while still disagreeing with him, and some explicitly challenging him and accusing him of leading a group of users referred to mockingly as 'yokeimites'. The user kelsofabulous, also a fierce critic of Yokeup, referred to him mockingly as 'Jeffy' and regularly and publically criticized him. This issue of Javid's 'Latasha' story displaced the explicit discussion of theology as the most important issue in interactions between Christian and atheist/non-religious users and reoriented my observation from looking at disagreement and dialogue between Christian and atheist/non-religious users as the primary locus of affiliation and grouping. In the course of 2008, disagreements between Christians appeared to be more regularly the result of differences in personality, race, and physical location rather than theology.

The 'Latasha mystery' served a priming function for the drama episode from which the main videos that have been analysed in this project have been taken. The videos appearing at the end of 2008 often have reference to Javid and Yokeup's disagreement, although by this time both had generally stopped addressing each other directly. Several atheist/non-religious users had come to Javid's defence and had called him a friend. Both Crosisborg and TOMMYfromtheBRONX were also friendly with jezuzfreek, and jezuzfreek, although also an Evangelical Christian, interacted with both users on and off YouTube. Yokeup felt that this was inappropriate behaviour for Christians and attacked jezuzfreek for his relationships with the atheist/non-religious users, as well as with Javid. In December of 2008, Yokeup began to argue with the atheist user Crosisborg, who, in the escalation of the argument, maligned Yokeup's wife, particularly her claim to be a reformed lesbian. Yokeup made a video in which he responded angrily, insulting Crosisborg and those aligned with him, calling Crosisborg 'human garbage'.

The drama analysed in this book began with an argument between Crosisborg and Yokeup in which insults were exchanged. There was a long history of drama between Crosisborg and Yokeup, which developed from Yokeup's condemnation of Christians who were friendly with Crosisborg and his argument that Christians should not be friends with atheists. At one point in their interaction in late 2008/early 2009, Crosisborg made a video that included joking about Yokeup's wife, calling her a 'lesbian' and making negative comments about her sexuality. This was offensive to Yokeup and Caroline because Caroline's story of conversion to Christianity included a claim that she had changed her sexuality, having previously been involved in a relationship with a woman before converting. By calling her a 'lesbian', Crosisborg rejected Caroline's own description of herself and insulted Yokeup by appearing to challenge both the validity of their relationship and Yokeup's own masculinity.

In response, Yokeup called Crosisborg 'human garbage', and after great outrage from others, Yokeup argued that he had only called Crosisborg 'human garbage' because all non-Christians were 'human garbage', using the parable of the vine and the branches from John 15 to support his argument. The initial videos that both Crosisborg and Yokeup made were subsequently removed and were not online at the time of data collection, although two atheist users did download Yokeup's videos and reused elements of these (including video and images) in their own videos. This enabled some reconstruction of what Yokeup had said in the initial interaction with Crosisborg. Yokeup potentially made several videos about 'human garbage' that were subsequently taken down. theoriginalhamster's video entitled 'yokeup the crackwhore' presents a remix of a video made by Yokeup in the morning outside of his house. Yokeup appears to be extremely agitated, speaking loudly, aggressively, and insultingly toward Crosisborg and jezuzfreek. philhellenes' (pronounced phil-hell-ains) video 'YouTube's Psychopath: Yokeup.' includes audio from Yokeup videos in which Yokeup appears to use the term 'human garbage' and 'human garbage dumps' several times.

Yokeup and Crosisborg took down the most intense videos they made, but the phrase 'human garbage' continued to be referenced in subsequent videos. Although the original insulting videos did not remain, the residue of the disagreement remained, particularly in Crosisborg's calmer responses, which were still available on his channel at the end of the observation period. Yokeup, rather than apologizing and claiming to have misspoken, made a video claiming that the term 'human garbage' was taken from John 15 in which Jesus describes fruitless branches as being cut away and thrown into a fire. Yokeup appeared to have made this video once initially in January 2009, deleted it, and made another video clarifying his argument on 13 February 2009.

The videos made in response to 'human garbage' focused both on the inappropriate nature of Yokeup's actions, but also his interpretation of John 15, which several Christian users felt was inappropriate. In both the atheist and Christian communities, disagreement over what response should be made to the use of the term occurred. In the atheist community, although the term was not defended by anyone, PaulsEgo argued that Yokeup was representing the true form of Christianity and should be encouraged to continue to make videos. Others, particularly Crosisborg who was friendly with other Christian users, felt that Yokeup needed to be denounced by both Christian and atheist/non-Christian users. Within the Christian community, significant debate also occurred which contributed to some of the alliances that had been built during the controversy surrounding Javid. At the time many Christians questioned Yokeup's interpretation of John 15, claiming that Jesus had intended for the parable in John 15 to be only addressed to Christians. The denouncements came, however, with some caveats about the need for Christians to 'preach the truth' about hell and judgement.

Although few videos were made in support of Yokeup, evidence that others agreed with him can be observed in the comments sections of his videos. A video made by another user on Yokeup's collaborative Christian channel souledouttojesus in 2010 also showed support for Yokeup's use of the term, although the particular user posting on the channel said he was not comfortable using the term himself (souledouttojesus, 2010). Importantly, there seemed to be a difference in the image that 'human garbage' produced among users. For Yokeup, he referred back to the image of branches being burned, but other users, including philhellenes and commenters on his video, implied that the term brought images of the burning bodies and the Holocaust.

The episode surrounding the 'human garbage' term appeared to be an instance in which users could be seen as either supporting Yokeup's brash and confrontational style as 'preaching the truth', or denouncing him and his ministry as being misguided and too harsh. For Yokeup and those who supported him, the issue was rooted in whether or not Christians were willing to take unpopular opinions supported by the Bible (particularly their interpretation of the text).

In September of 2009, Yokeup and several users who were the most strongly opposed to him and his ministry met in a chat room and decided that, although they disagreed with one another, the appearance to atheist/non-Christian users watching their videos was that Christian users were constantly bickering with one another. In an attempt to help overcome this impression, they decided to stop explicitly attacking one another, and Yokeup in particular stopped his regular practice of 'calling out' other Christian users. Disagreements about the term 'human garbage', however, could be seen throughout 2010 as Yokeup continued to use the term and make the same defence rooted in his interpretation of John 15. In the summer of 2010, videos made by PeaceInChristAlone and Yokeup's responses showed that the term continued to cause similar responses from Christian users: that although the truth of the gospel needs to be preached, some care must be taken in how the gospel is presented to non-believers. Yokeup continued to argue, however, that it was necessary to produce a harsh accounting of the 'reality of the gospel' to non-believers so they will not be deceived into believing that they will not face a harsh judgement.

YouTube videos as data

After having observed the 'human garbage' drama as it occurred between January and June 2009, in the summer of 2010, I initially identified 40 videos that appeared to be both related to the 'human garbage' drama and remained posted on the site. Starting with a search for the term 'human garbage', potential videos related to the topic were identified from appearing in the search and from examining responses to these videos and videos made around the time of the controversy.

After the 40 videos were identified as potentially having some relation to the 'human garbage' drama, I initially watched all the videos and read all the comments. I then focused on videos made in relation to the initial controversy (i.e. Yokeup's first uses of 'human garbage', the initial responses, and his subsequent defence of the term) and discarded videos that did not ultimately relate to the drama. Twenty videos posted either near the time of the initial controversy or reposted later were therefore identified for analysis (see Appendix for full list of videos). Within the 20 videos, three specific exchanges between users (i.e. videos and responses) were further identified for close discourse analysis. The three drama exchanges represented three different kinds of interaction: Christian and atheist; atheist and atheist; and Christian and Christian. Collecting a large corpus of data and identifying specific videos within the corpus for close discourse analysis allowed both for a macro-level description of discourse throughout the whole of the 'human garbage' drama (particularly as it related to use of systematic metaphor) and for a micro-level description and analysis of actual instances of interaction (particularly as it related to metaphor, categorization, and positioning). Findings at both levels of analysis could then be compared and combined, providing a full description of the interaction.

Twenty video pages from the 'human garbage' drama were included for analysis. Table 2.1 presents key information about the whole of the corpus. The data was collected in August of 2010, some 15–19 months after the videos had been initially posted, and comment and view counts were accurate at the end of the data collection period. However, because comments can be deleted and/ or posted as long as the video is online, counts can and do change over time. The videos in the video page corpus were all posted from 12 January–15 May 2009. 'Re: "Human Garbage" – searing TRUTH' (V20) was a reposted video (dated 8 September 2009), but the content of the video suggests that it was originally made in early May 2009.

Written text also contained automatically generated text, including nine words for every comment (the username of the commenter and the timestamp of the comment in relation to when the video was being viewed). There were also eight automatically generated words per video (information about the date and username). This automatically generated text was included for informational purposes about who had commented on a video and the chronological order of the comments, but will be excluded from analysis and excluded in calculation of metaphor density and distribution.

Videos varied in length, with the shortest video in the dataset playing 3 minutes and 31 seconds and the longest playing 10 minutes and 45 seconds, with a mean length of 6:47. The numbers of views and comments on videos

Table 2.1 Video page corpus

Number of video pages	20
Period of video posting	12 January–15 May 2009
Total video length	2:15:42 (hrs:mins:secs)
Total words	86,859
Video transcript text	23,582
Written text	63,277
Range of video lengths	3:31–10:45 (mins:secs)
Total number of comments	1,738
Range of comments per video	1–613
Range of views per video	102–17,510

varied more substantially. The most-viewed video, entitled 'YouTube's Psychopath: Yokeup.' (V5), had 17,510 views and 613 comments at the time of data collection, while the least-viewed video, entitled 'Re: "Human Garbage" – searing TRUTH' (V20), had 102 views, and the video with the fewest comments, 'Human Garbage … Are YOU? (My Response)' (V4), had only one comment at the time of collection.

Of these 20 videos, three exchanges (i.e. videos and responses) were identified for close discourse analysis. The total length of these videos was 31 minutes and 58 seconds, with a total of 1,043 comments and 41,176 words, including all elements of the video page as well as the transcripts of video talk.

- In the first exchange, Yokeup's initial video was removed soon after it was posted, but audio of the video was included in atheist philhellenes' 'YouTube's Psychopath: Yokeup.' (V5) in which Yokeup can be heard using the term 'human garbage' and arguing that the Biblical parable of the vine and the branches from John 15 supported his use of the term. Responses to Yokeup's video by other users suggest that the title of the video was 'Human Garbage … Are YOU?' and that it was posted between 10 and 13 January 2009. Audio and images from another video that Yokeup made during this time were extracted and remixed by theoriginalhamster in a video entitled 'yokeup the crackwhore' (V1). Both theoriginalhamster and philhellenes' videos, and Yokeup's subsequent argument in the videos entitled 'are YOU garbage in GOD's eyes?' (V11) and 'more on … human garbage' (V14) were, therefore, used in the analysis to recover the tone and content of the missing videos. In response to Yokeup, Crosisborg posted a video entitled 'Yokeup: Poster Boy for Bad Christians' (V3) on 14 January 2009 arguing that Yokeup's 'bad behaviour' was unacceptable and calling on other users, both atheists and Christians, to condemn Yokeup.
- In response to Yokeup's initial use of 'human garbage', philhellenes' 14 January 2009 video entitled 'YouTube's Psychopath: Yokeup.' (V5) was made immediately after Yokeup's initial video and contains the extracted audio mentioned above. In the video, philhellenes angrily responded to Yokeup calling him a 'psychopath'. PaulsEgo responded with the video entitled 'A spotlight.' (V6). In this video, PaulsEgo argued that although

Yokeup's talk had been offensive, Yokeup's offensive language was ultimately positive because Yokeup represented 'real' Christianity and his offensive talk illustrated what was 'so bad' about Christian belief.

- In the final exchange, christoferL posted a video entitled 'John 15 for Dummies – Unbelievers are human garbage?' (V12), which implicitly challenged Yokeup's exegesis of John 15 and argued that because the parable of the vine and the branches was directed at Jesus' disciples, it could not be used to describe the judgement of 'non-believers'. In response, Yokeup posted a video entitled 'more on . . . human garbage' (V14) in which he also questioned christoferL's exegesis of John 15 and reasserted his argument that his words were supported by the Bible. He also argued that 'people like christoferL' were more eager to be popular on YouTube than to follow the Bible.

In discussing the data, I follow these conventions:

- Users are referred to in the way they are best known on YouTube. In most cases, this is a username, while in others it is a first name or nickname. Users may choose to capitalize different characters in their usernames for stylistic purposes, and I use the capitalization the user has employed even at the beginning of a sentence. For example, user christoferL and Yokeup employ different capitalization conventions.
- Individual video's pages are referenced by their position in the 20 video page corpus of data analysed for the project. Information about the videos (including their URLs) can be found in the Appendix. The numbering of videos follows their chronological order, with V1 being posted prior to V2 and so forth.
- Text comments from videos have been reproduced in their original forms with all typographical errors, alternative spellings, lack of capitalization, and grammatical inconsistencies left unchanged.
- I have maintained differences in spelling from original texts (both academic texts and comments) without notation.
- The terms 'Christians' and 'atheists' are used to maintain a distinction between users who explicitly professed a belief in the Christian God and those who proclaimed themselves 'atheists' at least once in the period of observation. Users who did not self-proclaim a belief are not labelled.

Ethical considerations

In CMC research, despite longstanding debate over the ethical issues of using online content in research, the consensus continues to be that public texts are free to use without consent while private texts require consent (Frankel & Siang, 1999; Herring, 1996; King, 1996; Morris, 2004; Walther, 2002). On YouTube, users can post a video privately or publish it publicly on the site. YouTube states explicitly in their user policy, 'Any videos that you submit to the YouTube Sites may be redistributed through the Internet and other media channels, and may be viewed by the general public' (YouTube, 2008). YouTube also explicitly states copyright policy: 'When you create something original, you own the copyright for it. Likewise, when other people create content, they may have a copyright to it. As a creative community, it's essential that everyone on YouTube respect the copyrights of others' (YouTube, 2008). According to YouTube policy, YouTube videos are therefore protected and subject to the laws and rules surrounding the use of copyrighted materials.

When I undertook my research, I followed the British Association of Applied Linguistics guidelines on good practice for using internet texts, which state that 'in reaching a decision on consent, researchers need to consider the venue being researched, and any site policy on research and informants' expectations. In the case of an open-access site, where contributions are publicly archived, and informants might reasonably be expected to regard their contributions as public, individual consent may not be required' (British Association of Applied Linguistics, 2006:7). YouTube videos are public and subject to copyright law and, therefore, do not require informed consent. In terms of reproduction of images and texts, use of copyrighted material for research purposes is protected by fair use law in the United States (United States Code, 1976), where many of the videos originate, and by fair dealing laws in the UK (Copyright, Designs and Patents Act 1988, 1988), where the research was primarily carried out.

With regard to the potential for harm to the participants that might occur from analysis of their videos, the videos analysed in this project were all made by adult users who appeared to be aware of YouTube policy about the publicly accessible nature of their work. Although their public position does not guarantee that users would not suffer harm from analysis of their videos, it does appear unlikely. Care was taken in the analysis not to favour any position in the 'human garbage' drama and to present all users with respect and deference. Given the nature of drama interaction, particularly the hateful descriptions of others, I also considered whether or not my analysis might give further voice to the antagonistic language contained in videos. Although I recognize the potential for hateful language to be spread with the dissemination of this research, its value in elucidating how disagreement and misunderstanding occurs between people of different beliefs and faith backgrounds outweighs the potential harm from repeating and reproducing the discourse. The value of this kind of research on inter-faith dialogue can be seen in the publication of my earlier work in the practitioner journal *The Journal of Inter-Religious Dialogue* (Pihlaja, 2010), and in comments made on the popular US-based political blog 'The Huffington Post' (Stanton, 2010) about the application of my research.

Discourse analysis

Given the rich set of opportunities for discourse and social interaction available on the YouTube page, adapting a set of analytic tools to account for all video page elements is a necessity for analysing interaction on the site. Rather than being a static, textual artefact that can be extracted and analysed, YouTube video pages change over time. Users can post and take down videos whenever they choose, often resulting in different videos being available for analysis at different times. Analysis of YouTube drama must then take into account not only the videos that are available for analysis, but other videos that may have appeared and been subsequently removed.

After the videos were identified, I transcribed the spoken language using intonation units (Chafe, 1994), following a full description of this methodology in Stelma and Cameron (2007). After the video talk was transcribed, I segmented the transcribed text for close discourse analysis, following the procedure presented by Cameron and Maslen (2010a). Each segment represented a discourse action in the video, including greetings, introductions of topics, and closings. I segmented the videos when one or more of the following occurred:

- pauses
- discourse markers that explicitly signal a move to new activity (e.g. 'so' or 'now')
- changes in topic
- changes in address.

Following transcription and segmentation, all additional written text from the video page, including the video title, description, and tags, was copied into a Word document containing the video transcript and comments and then imported into the qualitative analysis software Atlas.TI (Muhr, 1993–2011). Atlas.TI enables analysts to gather large amounts of qualitative data into a single, searchable database, after which 'codes' or labels can be attached to words, images, videos, or extract of texts. Codes then can be organized into 'families' of related codes and queries can be made to investigate co-occurrence of codes or relationships between codes. I first coded all the participants and individuals that were mentioned on the video pages. This included all users who made comments, any reference to a user in a video or comment, and/or any reference to any individual either real or fictional throughout the whole of the dataset. Users who were known by more than one name or username (e.g. Yokeup, who had additional usernames including YokedtoJesus, and occasionally used his real name, Jeff) were included as a single representative code.

To track the 'antagonistic debate' of YouTube drama, I drew on the research into impoliteness reviewed in Chapter 1. Angouri and Tseliga's (2010) analysis of impoliteness in interaction in two online communities provided a useful example of research that balances analysis of micro-level interaction with the analysis of macro-level phenomena. In their work, 'impolite talk' was considered on several levels, from the spellings of individual words to analysis of interaction over time, including messages and responses. Their findings then show how im/politeness is 'embedded in the micro (discourse) and macro (social) context' (2010:57), making a connection between individual instances of discourse and the situated, unique social reality that interaction creates for users in a particular environment.

In drama, however, the whole of interactions between users could be described as 'impolite', but to analyse how each of the constituent elements contributed to the overall phenomenon, I looked at each interaction in the video corpus and followed this procedure:

1. Identify impoliteness in discourse:
   a. speaker reports an impolite intention; and/or
   b. uptake indicates hearer has taken offence from speaker's words; and/or
   c. speaker's words take the form of impolite language occurring elsewhere in the dataset.
2. Categorize forms of impoliteness.
3. Describe how users respond to impoliteness and how these responses developed into drama.

To describe impoliteness, I adapted the forms compiled in Hardaker (2010). Although Hardaker's study of 'trolling' is fundamentally different in both aim and scope (as she attempted to produce an academic definition of an emic, user term), employing previous descriptions of impoliteness to describe interaction within YouTube serves as a useful starting point for credible distinctions about user interactions. I also chose to adapt the descriptions to take into account Culpeper's (2011) description of impoliteness and concerns about intention:

- *Malicious impoliteness*: A user's behaviour (i.e. words and/or actions) explicitly conveyed the intent of causing offence and others viewed the behaviour negatively.
- *Non-malicious impoliteness*: User behaviour was presented without malice, but the speaker conveyed an anticipation that the behaviour may cause offence and attempted to mitigate it.
- *Mock impoliteness*: User behaviour was offensive in a friendly way without the presentation of malicious intent, and the behaviour was not viewed negatively by others.
- *Failed politeness*: A user's behaviour had an absence of appropriately polite behaviour, but the user did not convey an awareness that their behaviour may be perceived as impolite.
- *Failed malicious impoliteness*: A user presented their actions as attempting to cause offence, but others did not recognize it as such and, therefore, did not take offence.

- *Thwarted impoliteness*: User behaviour was offensive and the user presented malicious intent. Others, however, frustrated or thwarted the impolite behaviour, by not being offended, and/or either taking no action, or countering with sarcasm, contempt, or amusement.

Rather than attempt to deduce the intention of a speaker, I only analysed how a user portrayed their own intention and/or how others perceived their intention. I employed a confirmable approach of describing impoliteness by focusing on reports of, and responses to, actions and words that were viewed negatively by users and checking for empirical evidence of either user awareness of causing offence and/or others taking offence. For example, 'malicious impoliteness' could occur when a user was aware their words and/or actions would be viewed negatively, but made no attempt to mitigate the perception and the words and/or actions were viewed negatively. Examples of this were most frequently seen in comments where negative evaluations of others, such as 'Yokeup is an idiot', did not attempt to mitigate the perception of the comment. Conversely, 'non-malicious impoliteness' was identified when a user conveyed that they were aware their words and/or actions may cause offence and made an attempt to mitigate the offence. For example, in PaulsEgo's response to philhellenes, he said that he did not want his disagreement with philhellenes to be viewed negatively, but anticipated that others might view it in this way. I included all forms from Hardaker's list, but no clear examples of 'failed impoliteness' nor 'failed malicious impoliteness' were identified. Because the potential of these impoliteness forms to occur within YouTube drama appeared possible, I included them in my procedure to maintain a transferable analytic process.

I took into account both reports of intention to cause offence by the speaker and evidence in the uptake of respondents or commenters that the words and/or actions of another user were viewed negatively. This categorization was, however, dynamic and dependent on the context in which a stretch of talk or comment occurred. Shifts were identified when the same words and/or actions were presented or heard differently in the course of interactions. For example, Yokeup's initial categorization of the Crosisborg as 'human garbage' was 'malicious impoliteness' because of the offence present in Crosisborg's uptake and because no evidence in Yokeup's talk or response to Crosisborg suggested that Crosisborg had reconstructed Yokeup's intent wrongly. However, in subsequent uses of 'human garbage', Yokeup's use of the term was non-malicious impoliteness because he recognized the term might cause offence, and attempted to mitigate it by claiming the term was not his own, but derived from the Bible. The different presentations and uses of the same term meant that the form of impoliteness changed.

Having identified where in the discourse drama was occurring, I undertook another level of analysis, looking specifically at the use of language to trace the development of drama. To do this, I employed the following forms of discourse analysis:

- Metaphor-led discourse analysis (Cameron & Maslen, 2010b) will be used to investigate how user 'ideas, attitudes, and values' (Cameron, Low, & Maslen, 2010) are evidenced in language use, focusing on how micro-level metaphor use in stretches of discourse on individual video pages emerges as macro-level systematicity, both in systematic metaphor and metaphorical stories. Metaphor analysis will be used to show how metaphor use contributed to the beginning of drama.
- The reconsidered model of membership categorization analysis (Housley & Fitzgerald, 2002) will be used to describe individual instances of categorization in discourse, and patterns of categorization, and how categorization perpetuated the drama.
- Harré and van Langenhove's (1998) 'positioning theory' will be used to discuss how users then position themselves in larger storylines of conflict in the drama.

General searches of three additional resources were used when contextualizing terms and concepts that emerged in the discourse in the community. First, using the website Bible Gateway (www.biblegateway.com), various translations of the Bible were searched when Biblical language was used explicitly or implicitly in the user discourse. Second, the free online version of the British National Corpus (n.d.) as well as the Corpus of Contemporary American English (n.d.) were also consulted on occasion to investigate conventional use and compare the frequency of terms in the dataset with general usage. Third, general searches of the internet using Google as well as Wikipedia were also employed to investigate conventionalized use of terms, general surveys of Christian (particularly Evangelical) theological positions, and brief introductions to belief systems and religious movements that are referenced in the dataset.

The following chapters will then highlight each of these levels of analysis: metaphor in interaction, metaphor and categorization, and metaphor in positioning.

3

Withered Branches and Human Garbage:
Biblical and Metaphorical Stories

In the previous chapter, I told the story of Yokeup calling Crosisborg 'human garbage' and the trouble this created in the community. The action of insulting Crosisborg was one thing, but Yokeup's insistence that the term 'human garbage' came from the Bible, from the parable told by Jesus in the gospel of John, escalated the drama. Instead of discussing whether or not Yokeup's insult was acceptable or not, the question became about how a person can and should use the scripture. The whole of the drama revolved around the use of metaphor from the Bible and whether or not Yokeup's interpretation of the scripture was appropriate. To fully understand how and why metaphor contributed to the drama, an understanding of what metaphor is and the role it plays in interaction is required.

The discourse dynamics of metaphor

The prevalence of metaphor in thought and speech has been well documented (Cameron, 2003; Cameron & Maslen, 2010b; Gibbs, 1994; Lakoff & Johnson, 1980; Low & Cameron, 1999; Steen, 2007) and significantly different frameworks for investigating metaphor have developed in the last thirty years. Although various definitions of metaphor exist within these different approaches, as a starting point, a definition of 'metaphor' is useful in framing this research. I use 'metaphor' to describe the process of 'seeing something in terms of something else' (Burke, 1945:503), in language and, potentially, in thought (Cameron & Maslen, 2010b). Metaphor is indicated by a 'focus term or vehicle' in the text or talk which is incongruous with the surrounding text or talk and context, and in which the incongruity can be understood by some 'transfer of meaning' between the vehicle and the topic (Cameron, 2003).

In the insult that began the drama, Yokeup called Crosisborg and others 'human garbage'. This insult formed the metaphor 'Crosisborg is garbage', in which 'Crosisborg' was the topic and 'garbage' was the vehicle. By using the metaphor, Yokeup was encouraging others to view and understand Crosisborg in terms of something from the physical world about which most viewers would have negative connotations. The interesting thing about the use of the metaphor, however, was how it continued to be used and interpreted in the discourse that followed, with Yokeup using the Bible to explain his use of the metaphor (using more metaphorical language), and how the negative connotations attached to the word 'garbage' led to users employing new metaphors to respond back to Yokeup.

To analyse this dynamic use of metaphor requires a model of metaphor that takes into account how metaphors develop over time in interaction. Drawing on complex systems theory, a discourse dynamics approach to metaphor employs the notion of metaphor entering and remaining active in talk, treating it as 'a temporary stability emerging from the activity of interconnecting systems of socially-situated language use and cognitive activity' (Cameron, Maslen, Maule, Stratton, & Stanley, 2009:64). Emerging out of the complex system of situated language use, metaphor is then a phenomenon that develops in 'discourse activity' (Larsen-Freeman & Cameron, 2008), a claim supported by empirical research (Cameron, 2010b; Tay, 2011; Zanotto, Cameron, & Cavalcanti, 2008). Cameron and colleagues (Cameron & Maslen, 2010b; Cameron et al., 2009) have investigated the discourse dynamics of metaphor use in focus group discussions about the perceived threat of terrorism and shown how metaphor in the complex system of interaction among participants is 'processual, emergent, and open to change' (Cameron, 2009: 67). For example, speakers may employ the same metaphor vehicles in a stretch of talk or draw upon the related metaphorical language as they speak together.

This approach to metaphor contrasts with Lakoff and Johnson's (1980) influential conceptual metaphor theory, which has described metaphor primarily in terms of human cognition, suggesting that humans talk in metaphorical ways because they also think metaphorically. In this theory, conceptual metaphors are fixed mappings that are manifest in language and do not necessarily require understanding the context of the discourse because conceptual metaphors are said to be fundamental to human thought. Similarly, theories that emphasize the role of comparison of categories, including Glucksburg's class inclusion model of metaphor (Glucksberg & McGlone, 1999) and Bowdle and Gentner's 'career of metaphor' model (Bowdle & Gentner, 2005; Gentner & Bowdle, 2001), focus on the cognitive function of metaphor rather than the dynamic use of metaphor in interaction.

Ritchie (2010) notes, however, a recent shift from research into the relationship between thought and language in metaphor production and processing to a focus on metaphor in actual 'discourse activity', citing Charteris-Black (2005), Musolff (2004), and Cameron (2010a). In research into metaphor use in interaction, the focus is not on how individual speech and thought interact, but on how the interaction between speakers has important consequences for how metaphor is produced and meaning is negotiated. Ritchie, drawing on neurobiological research leading to perceptual simulation theory (Barsalou, 1999, 2008) and the work of Gibbs (2006), understands metaphorical and expressive language as activating entire conceptual schemas rather than fixed conceptual metaphors like those proposed in Lakoff and Johnson's work (Ritchie, 2006). Ritchie then argues, 'Since the simulations activated by a particularly expressive metaphor may remain activated for some time, if subsequent metaphors activate similar or compatible simulations the cumulative effect may be distinct from what could be accomplished by any one metaphor on its own, and may also be more enduring' (Ritchie, 2010:66). Metaphor, then, enters discourse and remains active in the interaction between speakers over time, dependent on the context of the interaction and the simulations that the language activates.

From a discourse dynamics approach, metaphor use can and does develop and change over time, affected by the particular constraints of a unique instance of interaction. Individual metaphor uses in interaction are not then treated as instantiations of conceptual metaphor, but as potential parts of a 'metaphor trajectory'. The notion of 'trajectory' is also taken from complex systems theory and describes the successive points that the system has occupied as forming a 'path' or 'trajectory' of states in the system's 'landscape of possibilities' (Thelen & Smith, 1994 cited in Cameron, 2010a:83). The tracing of a metaphor trajectory, then, can be used to show connections between metaphor uses throughout the discourse, where and when in the discourse metaphor use is occurring, and how different speakers are adapting and modifying metaphor throughout the course of interaction. Compiling this information can then show how metaphor use contributes to and is a part of the development of the discourse over time.

This view of metaphor fits well with the drama I described in the previous chapter. The drama and interaction I observed was reflexive, with the videos that users made and the terms and words they employed to describe others affecting how users subsequently talked about the same people. There was a clear connection between the videos, in terms of not only the content, but the words and metaphors they used. The use of 'human garbage' in the first instance had a subsequent impact on how users spoke about Yokeup. Mapping the development of metaphor drama over time, given its centrality in the drama, could then provide insight into how the drama developed.

Cameron (2008) describes the various changes and adaptations that are made to metaphors as discourse proceeds as 'metaphor shifting', which can occur in three forms:

- In vehicle redeployment, a new metaphor can be formed employing the vehicle term from another metaphor, but changing the topic. Tay (2011), for example, has shown how the vehicle 'journey' develops in a sample of talk about therapy, serving various purposes and holding different meanings dependent on who is employing the vehicle and its context. One form of vehicle redeployment is metaphor appropriation, which occurs when 'a participant [begins] to use a metaphor that had ... been the discourse "property" of the other speaker' (Cameron, 2010b:14). Cameron observes the constructive effects of appropriation in conciliation discourse in which one speaker 'owns' the metaphor of 'healing' in a conversation, but the term is eventually appropriated by another speaker. When appropriation occurs, the metaphor is explicitly the shared property of both speakers.
- In vehicle development, the vehicle term of a metaphor is repeated, relexicalized, explicated, and/or contrasted in the course of discourse (Cameron, 2010a). Cameron further defines four types of vehicle development: vehicle repetition, when a term is repeated in an identical or

transformed way; vehicle relexicalization, where a synonym or equivalent is used; vehicle explication, where a term is expanded, elaborated, or exemplified; and vehicle contrast, when an antonymic or contrasting term is used. Unlike vehicle redeployment, however, in vehicle development the topic of the metaphor stays the same.

- In vehicle literalization, a vehicle can become literal or metonymic, and the vehicle and topic become indistinguishable, rendering the metaphorical literal and vice versa. Cameron cites the metaphor vehicle 'sitting down with' as a 'bridge term' (Kittay, 1987:166) in conciliation discourse as an example of literalization in which 'the vehicle domain is brought into the topic domain, and the metaphor is shifted into the literal' (Cameron, 2008:58). 'Sitting down with' in the conciliation data that Cameron analyses comes to have a metaphorical and literal meaning, describing both a physical meeting between victim and perpetrator, but also a metaphorical recognition of the other and willingness to engage in an open and vulnerable way.

Building on the analysis of metaphor in interaction and tracing metaphor trajectories in discourse, Cameron has also shown that systems of metaphor use emerge in discourse, instantiated as 'systematic metaphors' (Cameron & Maslen, 2010b; Cameron et al., 2009). While a cognitive approach to metaphor works with conceptual metaphors such as ARGUMENT IS WAR and identifies instantiations of these metaphors in language, a discourse dynamics approach investigates how speakers use metaphor in interaction and how these uses emerge as systematic ways of speaking about topics. Cameron, Low, and Maslen define a 'systematic metaphor' as 'a set of linguistic metaphors in which [semantically] connected vehicle words or phrases are used metaphorically about a particular topic' (Cameron, Low, & Maslen 2010:127). Systematic metaphors may be limited to individual conversations or interactions, or may emerge in broader social contexts. For example, in Cameron and colleagues' (Cameron et al., 2009) work on the perceived threat of terrorism, focus group participants spoke about terrorism in terms of games of chance. The individual uses of metaphors, when considered together, form a systematic way of speaking, in the case of the focus group forming the systematic metaphor BEING AFFECTED BY TERRORISM IS PARTICIPATING IN A GAME OF CHANCE with systematic metaphors typed in small caps and italicized. This systematic way of speaking is the result not only of individual cognitive function, but contextual interaction among speakers.

Metaphor-led discourse analysis is then the process of metaphor analysis that is informed by a discourse dynamics approach to metaphor (Cameron & Maslen, 2010b; Cameron et al., 2009). This process of analysing metaphor begins with identifying metaphor in text and talk. After identifying metaphor, metaphor vehicles are then grouped by semantic relationships following an inductive, 'grounded' approach to coding. Semantic groups of metaphor vehicles are then formed. After the grouping of metaphor vehicles, the analyst then identifies vehicle topics and produces lists of vehicles related to a particular topic. The set of related metaphors is the 'systematic metaphor' which 'summarises metaphorical ways of expressing ideas, attitudes, and values' (Cameron & Maslen, 2010b:128).

After construction and analysis of systematic metaphors, a metaphor-led approach to discourse analysis then investigates the use of metaphor in stretches of 'discourse activity' (Cameron, 2010c). This analysis focuses on local discourse action, investigating how metaphor is used, particularly as it relates to the research focus. Because analysis of metaphor systematicity focuses on the use of metaphor vehicles related to topics, the analysis of metaphor in context investigates how metaphor use develops over time and what actions it accomplishes in discourse. As an example, Cameron (2010c) presents a metaphor analysis of a speech by former British Prime Minister Tony Blair, showing how patterns in Blair's speech built up a metaphorical scenario using RELATIONSHIP metaphors. Blair used this scenario to describe his relationship with voters and accomplish the key goal of repairing his image. By analysing how metaphor use interacted in the discourse, what action metaphor use accomplished could then be elucidated.

Cameron also notes that, in addition to patterns of metaphor use observed in systematic metaphors, 'Sometimes participants' metaphors fit into a narrative, construct a metaphorical story, or connect into a larger, coherent "metaphor scenario" (Musolff, 2004) because of our cognitive tendency to construct explanatory stories for our experiences, a partial story or scenario may invoke a larger story or scenario in hearers' minds' (Cameron, 2010d:11). Cameron draws an important distinction between two forms of narrative systematicity in metaphor use, 'metaphor scenarios' and 'metaphorical stories'.

'Scenarios', in Musolff's terms, allow people to 'not only apply the source to target concepts, but to draw on them to build narrative frames for the assessment of (e.g.) socio-political issues' (Musolff, 2006:36). In this sense, 'scenarios' are the narrative outworking of fixed cognitive mappings. 'Metaphorical stories', on the other hand, describe metaphorical narratives in specific stretches of talk and text: 'The point about a "metaphorical story" is that it recounts (rather than assumes), normally within a single text or discourse event, actions involving one or more participants in settings as, "stories in conversation"' (Cameron et al., 2010:139). Metaphorical stories 'occur within a single discourse event, and tend to be marked out by the speaker in various ways, so that the listener or reader will recognize that a story, however short, is being told' (Cameron et al., 2010:144). Although metaphorical stories can interact with scenarios, metaphorical stories do not necessarily assume or require an underlying conceptual mapping.

Approaching metaphor use in discourse does not exclude considering the cognitive processes involved in metaphor production and interpretation. Metaphor use in discourse is seen as a complex interaction between thinking and language use (Gibbs, 1994). Gibbs (2011) highlights this in a recent article suggesting that humans have an 'allegorical impulse', *allegoresis*, 'in which we continually seek to connect, in diverse ways, the immediate here and now with more abstract, enduring symbolic themes' (Gibbs, 2011:122). This 'allegoric impulse' could influence the development of systematic metaphor and metaphorical stories, as speakers draw on shared symbolic themes in their socio-historical context. Rather than see allegory as super-extended metaphor interpreted in a cognitive blend (as in Crisp, 2008), Gibbs argues that allegory exhibits a meaning-making tendency in humans and that interpretation in allegories is dynamic, a process of '"soft assembl[y]" in the moment of experience depending on state of person, environment and task' (Gibbs, 2011:129). Allegoresis is then a complex, dynamic process in which cognition is only one component and not necessarily the dominant one.

In addition to 'scenarios' and 'stories', allegoresis offers a useful description of metaphor use (and particular narrative systematicity that draws on exophoric texts or narratives) in interaction, not as an artefact with a clear beginning and end, but as a process. The enduring symbols and themes that people employ may also be instantiated as stories or narratives, or they may appear in single uses of metaphors. The process of allegoresis can be influenced by all the factors in a complex system and is not simply conceived of as a linguistic representation of a cognitive process. Tracing when 'abstract, enduring symbolic themes' are introduced in discourse and whether or not the same themes are then repeated and/or expanded upon in subsequent talk can, like the analysis of systematic metaphors, elucidate the trajectory of discourse. How users employ these themes and the extent to which they employ the same or different symbols in their interaction then potentially offers the possibility of tracing how agreement and disagreement among users develops, particularly if themes are, like metaphor, developed in user interaction.

Given the importance of users' expectations, knowledge, and values in the community, metaphor-led discourse analysis provides a key first step to describe and analyse user expressions of 'ideas, attitudes, and values' (Cameron & Maslen, 2010b:128) in discourse. Analysis of metaphor use and trajectories of metaphor in discourse has the potential to elucidate how different kinds of systems, including individual lives and socio-cultural groups, contribute to the discourse and, subsequently, the social world (Cameron & Maslen, 2010b). By investigating how users employ metaphorical language in their interaction, both similarities and differences in metaphor use will help elucidate why disagreement and misunderstanding may be occurring. Finally, when narrative systematicity is present in discourse, insights can be drawn about users' values and beliefs by investigating the enduring themes that they connect to their day-to-day experience.

Doing metaphor analysis

As a starting point for analysing discourse in the YouTube videos that comprise the drama I described in Chapter 2, I employed this 'discourse dynamics' approach to metaphor to trace how metaphor developed in the drama and what role it played in the antagonistic debate among users. As with any analysis of metaphor in discourse, however, the first key question to resolve was how to identify metaphor in the discourse. For this book, identification of metaphor followed a modified version of the Pragglejaz Metaphor Identification Procedure (MIP) (Cameron & Maslen, 2010a; Pragglejaz group, 2007), a procedure developed by a group of eminent metaphor scholars for use in a broad range of metaphor analyses.

The Pragglejaz MIP follows:

1. The researcher familiarises her/himself with the discourse data.
2. The researcher works through the data looking for possible metaphors.
3. Each possible metaphor is checked for:
   i.   its meaning in the discourse context
   ii. the existence of another, more basic meaning
   iii. an incongruity or contrast between these meanings, and a transfer from the basic to the contextual meaning.
4. If the possible metaphor satisfies each of the above, it is coded as metaphor, usually by underlining or listing.

(Pragglejaz group, 2007:3)

The key modification to this procedure is the identification of metaphor as vehicle term rather than only at the individual word level (Cameron & Maslen, 2010a). I used both the Oxford English and Merriam-Webster dictionaries to search for more basic meanings of words, and I identified metaphor vehicles in the dataset by underlining them. An example of the vehicles identification follows:

> I believe that a Christian's job is to work on their OWN life, before pointing out things to others, we SHOULD NOT JUDGE. I will not judge any of you.

In the extract, 'job', 'work', 'on', 'pointing out', 'things', 'to', 'JUDGE', and 'judge' were marked as metaphor vehicles. After piloting the metaphor identification of a single video page, consistency checks were performed by four metaphor scholars. This served as an informal inter-rater reliability check and discrepancies among vehicle identification were discussed before the procedure was undertaken on the remaining video pages in the dataset. In Chapter 5, metaphor vehicles are underlined in data extracts, and, unless obvious, when discussed in the text. Metaphor vehicle groupings and systematic metaphors will be presented in small italicized capital letters (e.g., CHRISTIAN BELIEF IS MENTAL ILLNESS).

The identification of metaphor initially proved difficult in marking vehicles in metaphorical stories, particularly those taken from the parables in the Bible. Where these metaphorical stories began and ended in the discourse was not always clear. Following the metaphor identification procedure, I constantly returned to whether or not a constituent element of a story had a more basic meaning when deciding to mark individual words as metaphor vehicles. I coded all metaphor vehicles using the qualitative analysis software, and chose to code individual metaphor vehicles in consolidated forms to preserve a manageable number of codes for the grouping of metaphor vehicles in the next stage of analysis. For example, I chose to use the singular form of words, such as 'lion' for instances of the words 'lions' and one code for all tenses of a verb, such as 'look' for 'looked' or 'looking'. This reduced the number of codes and allowed for simpler searches and groupings of codes. I also used single codes for phrasal verbs, compound nouns, and proper nouns rather than coding them as two more codes.

All prepositions that were used with potential metaphoric meaning were also marked in the dataset. Prepositions that collocated with metaphorical verbs were, in most cases, marked as metaphor as in pointing out ... to, and the commonly occurring collocations of remain in and look at. In instances where the verb was not used metaphorically, the preposition was normally not marked as a metaphor, with the key exception of believe in which occurred regularly in the dataset. Given the nature of the discourse in which users discussed Biblical metaphorical language at length, physical action was very rarely described.

Metaphor vehicles were then grouped together in 'code families' in Atlas.TI. The grouping of vehicles followed the process established by Cameron, Low, and Maslen (2010) to identify potential systematic metaphor use in the video transcripts and comments. In this process, metaphor vehicles are grouped together and labelled based on semantic field. For example, 'brilliance', 'glitter', 'sparkle', and 'enlighten' among other vehicles shared a semantic field of LIGHT and were, therefore, grouped together. The process of grouping metaphor vehicles cannot be, however, a totally objective process, and Cameron, Low, and Maslen (2010) emphasize the need for flexibility and recursion in grouping metaphor vehicles.

Initially, I grouped by semantic field, employing the categories used by Cameron and colleagues (2009) as shown in Table 3.1.

After initial grouping of the vehicles, I discarded several groupings which contained no vehicles (including HOME and HARD) and evaluated the OTHER grouping for patterns among vehicles potentially forming new groupings (see Table 3.2). I also considered the labels for the groupings from the list and

Table 3.1 Vehicle groupings

BALANCE	FOLLOWING-LEADING	PHYSICAL ACTION
BLOW	FORM	POINT
BODY-FOOD-CLOTHES	GAME	READING-WRITING
BUILDING	GIVING-TAKING	RELIGION
CIRCLE	HARD	SEEING
CLEAN-DIRTY	HOME	SORT
COMMERCE	HORIZONTAL (LANDSCAPE)	SOUND
CONCEALMENT	HOT-COLD	SPEAKING/LISTENING
CONCRETISING	INCLINE	STRENGTH
CONNECT-SEPARATE	LABEL	SUPPORT
CONSTRAINT	LOCATION	THEATRE/STORIES
CONTAINER	MACHINE	VIOLATE/LIMITS
CRAZY/WILD	MILITARY	WATER
DEPTH	MOVEMENT	COMPONENT PARTS
DIMENSION	NATURAL WORLD	THING
FEELING	NUMBER	EXPLETIVE
FINDING-LOSING	OPEN-CLOSE	OTHER

From Cameron et al., 2009.

Table 3.2 Vehicle groupings

BODY-FOOD-CLOTHES	FOLLOWING-LEADING	OPEN-CLOSE
BUILDING	FORM	OTHER
BURNING*	GAME	PHYSICAL ACTION
COMMERCE	HOT-COLD	READING-WRITING
COMPLETE	LAW*	RELIGION
CONNECT-SEPARATF	LIGHT*	SEEING
CONSTRAINT	LOCATION	SOUND
CONTAINER	MACHINE	SPEAKING-HEARING
DEPTH	MENTAL ILLNESS	STRENGTH
DISEASE*	MILITARY-WAR	THEATRE-STORIES
DIMENSION	MOVEMENT	THING
DIRTY-CLEAN	NATURAL WORLD	TIME*
FAMILY*	NAUTICAL*	VIOLENT ACTION
FEELING	NUMBER	WATER

renamed several to better fit the vehicles in the dataset. For example, I chose to label the grouping of WILD/CRAZY more precisely as MENTAL ILLNESS given the vehicles contained in the grouping. I also chose to group all EXPLETIVE vehicles in semantic groupings rather than have a separate grouping.

After identifying metaphor vehicles and grouping them, I attempted to identify the topics of the metaphor vehicles where possible. Although Cameron,

Low, and Maslen (2010) note that topics can be difficult to identify, particularly in spoken discourse, within the community, instances of explicit categorization of others employing metaphorical language often included a clear topic, such as 'Yokeup is a psychopath' and 'Crosisborg is human garbage'.

Biblical metaphor used to describe spiritual experience, however, proved particularly difficult in topic identification. Vehicles such as 'hearing God's voice' were used to describe spiritual experiences for which a concrete description is not made explicit. Biblical metaphorical language also presented difficulties when metaphor vehicles served as topics in metaphors quoted from the Bible, such as those in the parable of the vine and branches: remaining in Christ is being connected to a vine. A concrete topic for remaining in Christ is not present in the Bible and development of the vehicles in the discourse suggested that users again employed the term to describe a spiritual experience that could not be expressed as a concrete process.

To help resolve this issue, after identification of explicit topics, and following Cameron, Low, and Maslen (2010), a refined set of key discourse topics was developed, based on the aims and goals of the research. As this research aims to describe the development of YouTube drama, I chose topics that highlighted user responses to drama and evaluation of self and others' actions. The discourse topic of the drama was Yokeup's use of the term human garbage and his development of vehicles from the parable of the vine and branches to justify its use. Since all videos were made in response to this action, the data collection procedure limited the topics of videos and comments to how a user responded to Yokeup, how a user responded to another user's response to Yokeup, and/or how Yokeup's use of scripture either represented or misrepresented the Bible or Christian theology.

These discourse topics allowed me to deduce the topics of many of the ambiguous vehicles. Above, I mentioned how Biblical language such as 'remain in Christ' presented difficulties when attempting to identify topics. By investigating surrounding talk which included, for example, a positive response to another user's actions, concrete actions which were also described in tandem with the remain in vehicle could be used to identify a potential metaphor topic (e.g. loving others). Further, even when metaphors had explicit topics and vehicles (as in the case of 'Yokeup is a psychopath'), identifying the user talk about the actions associated with the vehicle showed how it was redeployed to new topics or used without an explicit topic in subsequent development. In the case of the psychopath vehicle, knowing which concrete actions were described in proximity to the vehicle's use showed the contextual meaning of psychopath. With this information, I was then able to analyse how individual metaphor use may have contributed to an emerging systematic metaphor.

Connections among vehicles identified in the video transcripts and comments were then considered and systematic metaphors were constructed, again following Cameron, Low, and Maslen (2010). I investigated metaphors in which 'connected vehicle words or phrases [were] used metaphorically about a particular topic' (Cameron et al., 2010:127). For example, after identifying the metaphor Yokeup is a psychopath in the user philhellenes' video entitled 'YouTube's psychopath: Yokeup', I investigated other vehicles in the MENTAL ILLNESS grouping, describing the systematic metaphor as CHRISTIAN BELIEF IS MENTAL ILLNESS. After constructing systematic metaphors in this way, I then compared results across the videos employing both the vehicle groupings and the metaphor density figures to see if the same or different systematic metaphor had emerged across the dataset or if it was limited to one or several video pages.

After identifying systematic metaphors and focusing on the aims and goals of the research, I analysed which metaphors contributed to the development of drama by considering systematic metaphor use in tandem with the additional discourse analysis of categorization, impoliteness, and positioning outlined below. Considering the research aims, I focused my analysis on systematic metaphors that were central to the 'human garbage' drama; that is, first, they contributed implicitly or explicitly to the 'antagonistic debate' among users; and second, they provided insights about user beliefs, values, and expectations, particularly in how they emerged from use by different individuals. I looked particularly at systematic metaphors that were used in disparate ways by opposing users (particularly users who were self-proclaimed Christians and those who were self-proclaimed atheists) to see what the metaphor use revealed about users' different positions.

After the initial grouping of vehicles by semantic field, I also grouped vehicles based on narrative systematicity, including vehicles which were constituent parts of metaphorical stories that were told explicitly in video talk and subsequently developed by users in comments and responses. In analysis of narrative systematicity and its role in drama, I focused on the action that metaphor accomplished, looking specifically at instances when metaphor shifting was contested or led to further disagreement among users. I also investigated if and how metaphors that showed narrative systematicity tied the immediate context to more 'enduring themes' (Gibbs, 2011) and whether or not the themes revealed anything about the users' own beliefs, values, and expectations about, in particular, social interaction on the site.

I exercised caution in this process because tracing metaphor use over time on YouTube can be difficult. Cameron and colleagues' (2009) used data from speakers in real time engaged in prolonged conversation, but YouTube discourse, and in particular vlogs in which one speaker addresses a camera without interaction with another user, does not include real-time interaction. Comments can occur after the posting of a video and are generally oriented towards the video talk, but users do not necessarily read others' comments or watch an entire video and caution must be taken in mapping connections and the 'trace' of a metaphor on a video page. Although the chronology of videos can be observed based on their posting date, the chronology of subsequent comments, and how many or which comments a user has read before posting their own comment, can be difficult to deduce. Commenters can also watch videos in any order after they have been posted, so a user may have watched a video posted on 2 February before watching a video posted on 30 January, and their comment could subsequently refer to both videos. To account for this difference in investigations of connections between metaphors, I adapted the analytic procedure to begin by identifying all the metaphors in video talk and then investigating whether or not the same metaphors and/or vehicles from the same groupings were used in comments rather than investigating metaphor use trajectory in comments sections.

In the process of grouping vehicles by semantic and narrative systematicity, a useful 'Bible' grouping emerged as particular to the dataset; that is, metaphor vehicles that alluded to or made explicit or implicit reference to the Bible. The process of constructing the grouping included identifying vehicles that were explicitly used in reference to the Bible (as in the reading of John 15 which occurred regularly in the dataset) as well as vehicles that did not have a direct reference, but appeared to be taken from the Bible. In these cases, I searched different versions of the Bible using an online resource, Bible Gateway (n.d.), to confirm if the vehicle was in the Bible and if the usage could potentially allude to the passage.

Biblical metaphor in Christian discourse

The video that began the drama, Yokeup's angry insult of Crosisborg as 'human garbage', was quickly removed, and the response videos by users in the community played out a common theme in YouTube communities, the reconstruction of what a person had said. On one side, Yokeup said he had just been telling the truth about what the Bible said, while on the other side, users accused Yokeup of being misanthropic and violent. Although posted a month after the initial drama, the video titled 'more on … human garbage' (V14) explicitly described Yokeup's position on how human garbage was developed from the John 15 text. In this video, Yokeup read from the text of the Bible and posted the text, taken from the King James Version of the Bible, in the video description.

> John 15.1–8
> 1 I am the true grapevine, and my Father is the gardener. 2 He cuts off every branch of mine that doesn't produce fruit, and he prunes the branches that do bear fruit so they will produce even more. 3 You have already been pruned and purified by the message I have given you. 4 Remain in me, and I will remain in you. For a branch cannot produce fruit if it is severed from the vine, and you cannot be fruitful unless you remain in me.
>
> 5 Yes, I am the vine; you are the branches. Those who remain in me, and I in them, will produce much fruit. For apart from me you can do nothing. 6 Anyone who does not remain in me is thrown away like a useless branch and withers. Such branches are gathered into a pile to be burned. 7 But if you remain in me and my words remain in you, you may ask for anything you want, and it will be granted! 8 When you produce much fruit, you are my true disciples. This brings great glory to my Father.

From a metaphor analysis perspective, the parable included the following metaphors: the disciples are branches, Jesus is the vine, and the father is the gardener. Within the parable, the following story was told: branches that remain in Christ, bear fruit and were pruned. Branches that did not bear fruit were cut and thrown away, and subsequently withered and were burned. The parable emphasized the importance of remaining in Christ and, therefore, showing oneself to be a true disciple of Jesus. The implication of the parable, further explicated in the following verses not included in the video description box (John 15.9–17), was that the hearer should follow Jesus' commands if they wanted to remain in Christ.

Before discussing how Yokeup interpreted the passage to support his position, it is important to briefly discuss the resource of the Bible in the Evangelical Christian faith which was most widely represented in the community I observed. The Bible, for Evangelical Christians, is not only an important text for living and deciding, it is the key authority on which their faith is founded, separate from the authority of any church denomination. Bebbington and Bebbington (1989) cite the noted Evangelical theologian J. I. Packer's (1978) work putting Biblical supremacy as the first in a list of Evangelical fundamentals. To exemplify the centrality of the Bible in Evangelical Christian belief, the following extract taken from the statement of faith of the influential American Evangelical denomination, the Southern Baptist Convention, is presented:

> The Holy Bible was written by men divinely inspired and is God's revelation of Himself to man. It is a perfect treasure of divine instruction. It has God for its author, salvation for its end, and truth, without any mixture of error, for its matter. Therefore, all Scripture is totally true and trustworthy. It reveals the principles by which God judges us, and therefore is, and will remain to the end of the world, the true center of Christian union, and the supreme standard by which all human conduct, creeds, and religious opinions should be tried. All Scripture is a testimony to Christ, who is Himself the focus of divine revelation.
>
> Exodus 24:4; Deuteronomy 4:1–2; 17:19; Joshua 8:34; Psalms 19:7–10; 119:11,89,105,140; Isaiah 34:16; 40:8; Jeremiah 15:16; 36:1–32; Matthew 5:17–18; 22:29; Luke 21:33; 24:44–46; John 5:39; 16:13–15; 17:17; Acts 2:16ff.; 17:11; Romans 15:4; 16:25–26; 2 Timothy 3:15–17; Hebrews 1:1–2; 4:12; 1 Peter 1:25; 2 Peter 1:19–21.
>
> (Southern Baptist Convention, n.d.)

In this definition, the 'Holy Bible' is described, not as a clear collection of writings in a particular book, but rather a series of properties. It is divinely inspired, authored by God, and totally true and trustworthy. This belief statement does not describe the actual, textual content of the Bible, but rather what is believed about it. The Southern Baptist Convention belief statement is not unique and other denominations and Evangelical organizations make similarly worded claims (Noll, 2001) showing an orientation to the Bible not as a particular book, but as a series of properties applied to a collection of texts that has been historically viewed as a central authority in Evangelicalism (Bebbington & Bebbington, 1989).

Malley's (2004) ethnographic work at an American Baptist church attempts to clarify what is meant by the 'Bible' in Evangelical Christian discourse, and highlights the difficulty that individual believers have in demarcating what is or is not the Bible. Malley proposes four conceptual elements of what Evangelicals mean when referring to 'the Bible':

1. A designation—"the Bible"—that can refer to various modern English Bibles.
2. An artifactual stereotype . . . that provides a recognition criteria for Bibles.
3. An assumption of textuality: the Bible is expected to be a text.
4. A presumption of common meaning: the various texts called Bibles are expected to have (basically) the same contents to say (basically) the same thing.

(Malley, 2004:67)

Like the Southern Baptist Convention belief statement, Malley shows that the Bible is also not necessarily conceived of as a particular book, but rather as what is contained within certain books, a 'common meaning' that can appear in different words at different times.

Because of the Bible's centrality in Evangelical Christian belief, Biblical interpretation is of particular importance for Evangelical Christians. A common description of the Evangelical Christian hermeneutic is 'Biblical literalism', the belief that the Bible is 'literally true' or 'infallible' (Bartkowski, 1996), which is often typified with literal understandings of the Biblical creation myth. This description of the Evangelical Christian hermeneutic, however, requires several important caveats. First, in practice, Evangelicals may concede that some elements of the Bible could be read figuratively, particularly language that is explicitly poetic or non-literal, as in the case of metaphorical language of the parables contained in the teachings of Jesus

(Malley, 2004). Second, a literal reading of the text does not ensure agreement among readers. As Bartkowski (1996) shows, disagreement among Evangelical Christians about corporal punishment of children is not resolved by a 'literal' reading of the text; instead, various readings evidence conflicting worldviews with which different readers approach the text. A description of Evangelical Christian understanding of the Bible as 'literal' does not, therefore, account for how and why disagreements arise between two readers applying the same hermeneutic.

This relationship between the reader and text, and how meaning is deduced, has long been of interest in reader reception studies, and Mailloux (1989) notes that theories of reader reception can generally be placed in two categories: 'textual realism', which sees readers as discovering meaning in texts; and 'readerly idealism', which sees readers as creating meaning from texts. Allington (2007) notes, however, that readers seek to avoid the impression that they are the originators of meaning. Although it is appropriate to interpret the text to find the original meaning, the meaning cannot be one that the reader has 'made up' for him or herself.

Malley's (2004) work shows the complex interaction of both finding and creating meaning in Biblical interpretation by Evangelical Christians, because although they may believe the Bible to be inspired by God and 'totally true and trustworthy' (Southern Baptist Convention, n.d.), they also believe God speaks to the believer and guides their reading (Nuttall, 1992). Evangelical Christian belief dictates 'textual realism', in which the meaning of the text is defined by God and Christians discover the meaning, but Evangelical Christian practice tends towards 'readerly idealism', in which the readers bring their own experiences and knowledge to bear on their interpretation of the text. Particularly in social settings like Bible studies, contextual factors can play a role in how the text is interpreted, and what knowledge is brought to bear in interpretation can differ depending on who is present in the immediate context.

These issues are particularly prescient in looking at Yokeup's interpretation of John 15 in the video 'more on … human garbage' (V14). He explicitly referenced the text in the video and read directly from the Bible passage, commenting like a preacher on the scripture throughout his reading. Although the term 'human garbage' was not contained in the parable of the vine and branches Yokeup presented the vehicle as a development of the parable's withered branches vehicle, saying that 'if you are not connected to Christ, if you not connected, you cannot bear fruit if you don't bear fruit, God prunes you, you wither in a pile, you are burned, you're—you're garbage.' Where the Bible verse ended and where Yokeup's own words began was therefore not explicitly marked and the commentary and the text ran together.

By presenting the text in this way, weaving the text with his own words, Yokeup drew equivalence between the metaphorical language in the parable and his own talk. He accomplished this by first relexicalizing 'remain in' Christ to be 'connected to' Christ and then implicitly redeploying the topic 'you' from the Biblical parable. Yokeup developed 'withered branch' from 'garbage' using 'wither in a pile' to illustrate the relationship between the words. Although the 'you' in the context of the parable was ostensibly Jesus' disciples, the text establishes a new topic for the vehicle 'branch' in verse six: 'Anyone who does not remain in me ...' (John 15.6), which Yokeup explicated as anyone who 'is not connected to Christ' to include contemporary readers of the text, using the generic 'you' as the topic for the metaphor 'you are garbage', and establishing an implicit metaphor 'anyone who does not remain in [Christ] is garbage'. The use of the topic 'you' also made the language of the parable more direct. Whereas the Bible referred only to 'anyone who does not remain in me' (John 15.6), Yokeup's retelling of the parable directly addressed the viewer and the parable was, in Yokeup's talk, not only about the burning of 'people who do not remain in Christ', but of the video viewer.

The presentation of himself in this way showed him giving an authoritative, original reading of the text, but in the case of interpretation of Biblical – in particular, Biblical metaphorical – language, privileged readings of the text, influenced by the power structures within which these readings are made, impact believers (Foucault, 1981, 1982). This 'pastoral power' of the church exerts influence over the life of the individual, a power that is 'embodied and crystallized' in an institution, but which can also be found outside of the institution (Foucault, 1982:791). In analysis of Evangelical Christian discourse like Yokeup's, however, the institutionalized church can be obscured by the belief in the transparency and universal accessibility of the Bible (Boone, 1989).

No central, hierarchical authority on Biblical interpretation exists (as in the Catholic and Episcopalian churches), and Evangelical Christian hermeneutic activity becomes a complex interaction among individual ideology, context, and institutionalized Bible readings. Analysing interpretation of Biblical metaphorical language in particular must, therefore, take into account other interactional factors beyond whether or not Christians share the same categorical label, attend the same church, or affirm the same statements of belief. To take these other components into account, situating belief about the Bible within a larger belief framework that includes having a 'personal relationship' with God, is essential. Although there is a democratic aspect to the Evangelical understanding of scriptural interpretation, certain powerful, second-order discourses do still emerge, instantiated in statements of belief and ritualized liturgical calls and responses (Forrester, 1981). Teachings of church doctrine, therefore, both formally and informally can instil in believers particular ways of reading the Bible that are salient for Christians across denominational lines.

From branches to garbage

In Yokeup's exegesis of the Bible and his use of John 15 to insult others, he was able to present his own words as the words of the Bible and to, as Foucault writes, 'say something other than the text itself' (1981:58). His videos made no clear demarcation between where the words of the Bible ended and where his own began, enabling the development of 'garbage' from 'withered branches' to be potentially heard as part of the Biblical text. From Yokeup's discourse alone, one would not be able to determine which vehicles are contained in the parable and which ones are the result of his own development. Yokeup's exegesis of the parable, therefore, showed how vehicle development from the text of the Bible could be used to extend the language of the parable to new vehicles through comparison of Biblical metaphorical terms with new metaphorical language. The development of the metaphorical language also appropriated the moral authority of the Bible to Yokeup's own words by taking on the 'pastoral power' (Foucault, 1982) that is present when the Bible is quoted.

Yokeup suggested that his description of others as 'garbage' should not be viewed negatively because he had only quoted the Biblical parable of the vine and the branches (John 15) and had not intended to hurt anyone. Yokeup made this argument in two videos, 'are YOU garbage in GOD's eyes?' (V11) and 'more on … human garbage' (V14). In both, he read aloud from the Bible before describing others as 'human garbage', explicitly linking his own words to the Biblical text. Yokeup said, 'John 15.6 where Jesus is telling his disciples that if you are not connected to Christ … you cannot bear fruit if you don't bear fruit. God prunes you. You wither in a pile; you are burned. You're—you're garbage'. The matter-of-fact tone Yokeup took, however, presented his words as not intended to offend by specifically acknowledging that 'human garbage' might potentially be viewed negatively, saying, 'You might not like the way I'm saying this'. Yokeup insisted that 'this is all red ink', or the exact quotation of Jesus from the Bible, rather than his own words, suggesting that he is not the source of the term and implying only an intention to tell others what was written in the Bible, not offend them.

Presenting 'human garbage' in this way justified its use by allocating to the Bible the offence the words had caused and suggesting it not be viewed negatively because it was the 'word of God'. Yokeup then argued that any negative responses to his words were actually negative responses to the Bible, and any offensive words aimed at him were misdirected. In this way, Yokeup subverted the negative response he received from Christians and non-Christians, taking the 'hate' as a sign of piety, that he was doing what God wanted him to do. As in the commenter huskyfan1982's description a 'good Christian', which included 'being hated by the world', any criticism that Yokeup received could then be presented as further proof that he was acting correctly and needed to persevere. I will discuss this more in depth in the next chapter on categorization.

Although the term 'human garbage' began as an insult towards Crosisborg, the term was used in different ways over time. By presenting his own words as an extension of scripture, Yokeup developed the term to be part of his exegesis, rather than an insult, and rejected attempts to change how he spoke about others. Yokeup's attempt to allocate his words to the Bible was, however, interpreted by atheists, particularly Crosisborg, philhellenes, and PaulsEgo, as evidence that Christians were willing to act offensively regardless of the consequences. Instead of treating the Bible as authoritative in the same way as Yokeup, the atheists used Yokeup's justification of his actions as further proof that he and other Christians were 'insane' and did not deserve to be heard in the community because they were willing to say anything if they believed that the Bible supported them.

Yokeup furthered redeployed 'garbage' in the videos that were taken down, using it to describe others as human garbage dumps (as heard in the audio extracts at the beginning of philhellenes' video entitled 'YouTube's psychopath: Yokeup.' [V5]). Garbage was then redeployed from 'people who do not remain in Christ' to 'agnostics, gays, lesbians, and homosexuals'. Yokeup then relexicalized the vehicle of 'piles into which the withered branches were thrown' (John 15.6) as 'dumps'. Drawing on the development of withered branches to human garbage, the 'piles of withered branches' were relexicalized as 'human garbage dumps', implicating many more users as the topic for the vehicle garbage, including anyone who did not identify themselves as remaining in Christ. Yokeup did not comment on the development of the vehicles or address in later videos the potential problems of using these words. Instead, Yokeup consistently presented his language as the word of God, and as maintaining the meaning as the Bible.

Despite these attempts to present himself in a positive way, Yokeup was challenged by other Christians in the community, particularly the user christoferL. In his video entitled 'John 15 for Dummies – Unbelievers are human garbage?' (V12), christoferL took issue not explicitly with Yokeup's development of human garbage from the Bible, but the redeployment of the topic you to the vehicle withered branches. christoferL read from the entire John 15 passage to further emphasize the accuracy of his exegesis. After reading from John 15.9–17, which emphasizes the hearer of the parable must 'obey [Jesus'] commands' to 'remain in [God's] love', christoferL said the following:

> Now, Jesus was telling them how to remain a branch in the vine which was by obeying his commands, something that only his followers do. When Jesus refers to the branches that do not bear fruit, that have dried up and withered only to be gathered up and burned, he was referring to believers who do not remain in him and go their own way. They part from his way and do things their own way. They ignore his teachings and justify their actions by saying they're doing God's work, but in truth they're deceiving themselves.

christoferL used the verses that follow the parable to further challenge Yokeup's exegesis and use of human garbage to refer to 'unbelievers'. In the same way that Allington (2007) found readers arguing about whether or not a textual quotation had been taken 'out of context' in another's interpretation, christoferL took into account the context in which the parable was told and argued that withered branches in the parable could only be applied to the topic 'believers who do not remain in Christ' and not 'unbelievers' because the parable was told specifically to Jesus' disciples. christoferL argued that because 'unbelievers' cannot be in Christ, they cannot become withered branches. The vehicle garbage therefore could not take the topic 'you' if the hearer was an 'unbeliever'. christoferL, therefore, did not explicitly challenge the development of garbage from the parable, but rather the redeployment of it to groups and people who might be considered 'unbelievers'. christoferL's video suggested that the problem was that the development did not maintain the original meaning of the parable, not that Yokeup's use of the term was wrong.

Although christoferL did not accept Yokeup's development of 'human garbage', he used the word 'burn' taken from the parable to refer to spiritual punishment in hell and specifically stated that, 'This isn't to say that unbelievers won't burn because unfortunately you guys you will if you don't accept Christ'. In this statement, christoferL affirmed his own belief in the Christian doctrine of hell, and the belief that 'people who do not accept Christ' will burn. The statement is ostensibly the same as Yokeup's assertion about human garbage that 'people who do not remain in Christ' will burn, but unlike Yokeup, christoferL did not suggest that any specific user would burn. Moreover, christoferL's use of the Christian term 'unbeliever' compared to Yokeup's use of 'agnostics, gays, lesbians, and homosexuals' also made the assertion that some people would burn less direct, since no users in the 'human garbage' drama self-identified using the word 'unbeliever'.

In repeated use of 'burning', the systematic metaphor SPIRITUAL PUNISHMENT IS BURNING appeared in the corpus, coming from the repeated references to John 15. When Yokeup retold the parable of the vine and branches in defence of his use of human garbage, he repeatedly emphasized the vehicle burn to describe the fate of unbelievers. Although the passage did not explicitly describe a Christian belief in hell, the presence of burn in the parable was used to compare the parable's burning with spiritual destruction in hell because both described spiritual judgement and punishment as burning. However, as with the other examples of Biblical metaphorical language, more concrete, non-metaphorical descriptions of this punishment were not present either in the 'human garbage' drama or the Bible, and it was unclear in Christian discourse whether or not they understood punishment in hell to include a physical burning or understood 'burning' as a metaphorical representation of punishment.

When christoferL and Yokeup employed descriptions of burning, no other Christians responding to their videos challenged their use of the metaphors, suggesting 'burn' was accepted as a vehicle for spiritual punishment among them. Moreover, although I have marked burn as a metaphor vehicle, in Christian talk and comments, the metaphoricity of the term might be questioned since belief in a literal hell with physical punishment persists in Christian belief and was observed in the course of my two-year observation of these users. In the video page corpus, however, this argument was not explicitly discussed, and there was no evidence in the discourse to suggest a definitive literal understanding of the term.

An accepted use of 'burning' to describe spiritual punishment after death among Christians did not appear to influence the understanding of 'burn' as spiritual punishment for other users, as evidenced by their development of the vehicle. Particularly for non-Christians, the use of burn with the object human garbage dumps in Yokeup's discourse appeared to index a literal burning of physical human bodies. philhellenes, in particular, developed 'burn' to semantically related vehicles, and literalized the vehicle in talk about the Holocaust, a process that was entirely absent in christoferL and Yokeup's talk about burning in the 'human garbage' drama context. When non-Christian users referenced hell and burning, some subverted the metaphor, suggesting, for example, that Yokeup should burn in hell, but the notion of burning as acceptable description of spiritual punishment was noticeably absent from non-Christian user talk.

christoferL followed the same pattern of attempting to present potentially offensive Biblical language as not motivated by an intent to offend others, but rather, simply the words of the Bible. In his video entitled 'John 15 for Dummies – Unbelievers are human garbage?' (V12), christoferL explicitly presented the belief that unbelievers would go to hell if they did not believe in God by saying, 'This isn't to say that unbelievers won't burn because unfortunately you guys you will if you don't accept Christ'. In this statement, christoferL carefully asserted a belief about the judgement of non-believers, but hedged the potentially offensive language by saying that the burning was 'unfortunate', attacking the face of 'non-believers' but with positive politeness (Brown & Levinson, 1987). In the same way as Yokeup, christoferL presented his words as not intended to offend, and although others might view his belief negatively, the Bible was the authoritative word of God and should be accepted. If anyone was subsequently offended, it was because the Bible had offended them, not christoferL. Unlike Yokeup, however, christoferL did so in a way that was presented as part of a larger narrative showing concern for 'unbelievers' rather than as an attack on another user without redressive action.

christoferL's treatment of language from the Bible about hell also showed the care christoferL took to balance community expectations about impoliteness and maintain relationships in the community. christoferL's video showed an awareness that for different users, different language could result in a negative attitude and, therefore, be considered impolite. Because no strong response to christoferL's presentation of hell was present, christoferL appeared to be successful in limiting the offence caused by his assertion that unbelievers would also burn. This lack of a negative response may have contributed to whether or not any others viewed the action negatively (or how offensive others thought his discourse was) since whether or not words or actions are viewed as offensive can depend on how others respond to words and/or actions (Lorenzo-Dus, 2009). Furthermore, when christoferL was mentioned in others' videos, no offensive language was directed at him. Christians in the comments section of the video praised christoferL's presentation of the Bible and his exegesis, showing his ability to maintain positive face with Christians as well.

The development of garbage from the parable of the vine and the branches was also opposed by other Christians who followed christoferL's reasoning. BudManInChrist (V13) and gdy80 (V20) as well as commenters appealed to other parts of the Bible to support their exegesis and to further interpret the meaning of the parable. Conversely, users who agreed with Yokeup also appealed to scripture to support Yokeup's exegesis and development of garbage. Acceptance of the term among Christians was in part contingent on whether or not they believed the development maintained the original meaning of the Biblical text. In the same way that Bartkowski (1996) showed that a 'literal' reading of the Bible did not resolve disagreements about corporal punishment because Bible passages supporting both sides of an argument can be offered, quotation of other parts of the Bible did not resolve the argument between Yokeup and christoferL.

The development of Biblical metaphor in non-Christian user talk

philhellenes' talk also appeared to suggest of a link between Yokeup's talk and Holocaust imagery, a theme that was reflected in the ways in which commenters on his video pages subsequently wrote about burning. Neither christoferL, Yokeup, nor the Christians who commented on their videos, however, appeared to recognize or address the literalization of 'burn' by philhellenes and others, and there were no instances in the data of the Christians attempting to clarify the meaning of burn.

Yokeup's development of human garbage from the parable resulted in a strong response from many users. In particular, the atheist philhellenes' video entitled 'YouTube's psychopath: Yokeup.' (V5) was the most-viewed video in the corpus and also had the most comments. philhellenes' video took audio clips of videos that Yokeup had posted, editing in the most offensive parts in a loop to make it sound as though Yokeup was repeating the same offensive words, particularly that people would 'burn' and the phrase 'human garbage dumps'. The image only showed white text on a black background, the text reading: 'Copyright free: For the purposes of parody, critique, common sense, human decency, sanity', followed by, 'Yokeup is a psychopath', 'You are listening to all the evidence I need', 'I could use images but that might distract from the audio', and finally, 'Listen'.

philhellenes appeared after the clips played, his head shown in black and white and looking directly at the camera, saying:

> When I saw this video . . . it's a video which provided the soundtrack that you just heard. I was thinking, how do I respond to that. 'Cause yeah, you're gonna get a response, Yokeup. And I thought about putting a glass plate [in] front of the video camera . . . And I mean I seriously thought about doing this . . . And waiting for you to do your diatribe . . . And then spitting at the camera. I can't think of any other appropriate response. You are fucking filth. You're a piece of shit. Talk about human garbage.

Unlike Yokeup's videos shot in the daylight, philhellenes video had a dark background and dim lighting, accentuating his aggressive physical presence. The image implied a face-to-face confrontation, with philhellenes standing up to Yokeup and taking a direct and clear stance against him.

In the video, philhellenes rejected the redeployment of human garbage dumps to 'Agnostics, Gays, Lesbians, and homosexuals', and presented himself as shocked and angered by Yokeup's words. philhellenes suggested that Yokeup's references to human garbage dumps burning was reminiscent of the Holocaust, drawing an implicit comparison between Yokeup and the Nazis and presenting Yokeup's talk as evidence that Yokeup lacked empathy for other humans and was, therefore, a psychopath. The use of metaphor in this way exaggerated negative evaluations of Yokeup with metaphorical hyperboles that presented Yokeup in the worst possible way. For philhellenes, the use of the term 'human garbage' did not lead to, as it did in christoferL's video, a discussion of whether or not Yokeup was interpreting the Bible in the correct way, but as evidence that Yokeup was a bad person, indeed a 'psychopath'.

At the centre of philhellenes response to Yokeup was a metaphorical story which mapped the interaction between Yokeup and philhellenes onto the tragic historical narrative of the sinking of the *Titanic*. In it, philhellenes further explicated the initial feelings he had when viewing Yokeup's video, presenting a story philhellenes told about Yokeup framed as a retelling a 'joke' about another Christian user named Geerup. philhellenes said:

> I once made a joke that if I was the captain of the Titanic and it was a choice between I think it was Geerup . . . I used the analogy with if it was a choice between Geerup and a puppy, nobody had to worry about the puppy. But after hearing this video, in all sincerity, the puppy would survive and you would have to be the best swimmer that the world has ever seen to survive Yokeup. And I mean it. I'd save a puppy before you. And anyone on the lifeboat who wanted to complain, they can complain all they like. I'll have no problem. I won't lose a moment's sleep.

philhellenes' story presents himself as the captain of the sinking *Titanic* and Yokeup as a passenger on the ship. In the metaphorical story, there is a full lifeboat and only one seat remaining. philhellenes must make a decision between a puppy that is also on the ship and Yokeup. philhellenes argued that he would choose the puppy rather than Yokeup without explicitly saying why. The story, therefore, described and explicated philhellenes' opinion that Yokeup was worthless, but in such a way that the opinion was a 'joke' rather than a concrete statement about Yokeup's real worth as a human.

Following philhellenes' talk, users also developed metaphor from the metaphorical story to describe Yokeup and their response to him. Of the 613 comments on the video page, thirty-six made reference to the metaphorical story, including six comments by philhellenes and thirty other unique users. In philhellenes' subsequent video entitled 'I Was Wrong' (V7), in which he clarified his statements about Yokeup, there were 109 comments, of which eleven explicitly referenced the metaphorical story, one of which was philhellenes' with ten other unique users. Two examples of commenters developing elements of the metaphorical story follow. ComradeAgopian wrote:

> Excellent response Phil. I for one would pick a cute puppy, stupid cat, or a flightless bird, over Yokeup. My only question would be did we get enough cold beer and sanwich's on the life boat.

And awormyourhonor wrote:

> I would choose the man. But the moment he said anything like "thank God" and started preaching to the boat. I would tell him to thank the rubber raft he was in, and probably kick him into the water with the yapping dog.
> I choose both.

Vehicle development within the metaphorical story occurred when the user ComradeAgopian suggested a substitution of the puppy for potentially less desirable animals. Additionally, the story was extended in time beyond the moment that philhellenes has ended it (with others in the lifeboat potentially complaining about the choice) to include other possibilities. In the extension of the story by awormyourhonor, Yokeup is taken on the lifeboat, but kicked out upon doing something more offensive. Similarly, in ComradeAgopian's extension, the need for food and supplies in the lifeboat is problematized. The comments show that the use of the metaphorical story encouraged users to also respond with metaphorical language, developing the same evaluation of Yokeup and his actions that philhellenes employed in his video.

Marking metaphor vehicles in these comments was challenging. Unlike philhellenes' story, which had a clear beginning and ending, the beginnings and endings of the metaphorical stories in comments that developed the vehicles were more obscure. Particularly in awormyourhonor's, in which Yokeup's preaching is taken into the metaphorical world of the story, the story's boundaries were not explicit. The vehicle development in both comments showed that my approach to marking vehicles was valid because users developed individual elements of the metaphorical stories in the same way as Biblically derived metaphors. In the development of each vehicle, user discourse further displayed beliefs and opinions about interaction in the context of the drama, supporting, extending, or opposing the original meaning of the story.

The *Titanic* story also served to present a moral question to the viewer about the relative worth of Yokeup's life. In philhellenes' telling of the metaphorical story, the choice of the puppy over Yokeup was explicitly resolved, but in response users engaged the question: who should be chosen to occupy the final seat in the lifeboat? The resulting discussion employed elements of the story to not only evaluate Yokeup, which was the initial purpose of the metaphorical story, but also to prime further discussion about the moral choice. awormyourhonor's comment highlights that the story encouraged users to consider Yokeup's actions and their own reaction to them in the same way that philhellenes had.

The tone of the initial telling of the metaphorical story also affected the tone of commenter response. After the story was presented by philhellenes as a 'joke' with comedic elements, comments were also often written in a 'joking' manner, with commenters producing comedic extensions of the story. For example, ComradeAgopian's comment made light of the hypothetical situation on the lifeboat, using a joking tone to ask whether or not there would be enough beer and food on the boat. Similarly, awormyourhonor's comment offers a comedic extension to the story in which Yokeup is kicked out of the boat and must swim with the 'yapping dog'. Although this comment also suggested some violence against Yokeup, as with philhellenes' joking use of violent imagery, the comment did not appear to be treated as a legitimate threat against Yokeup.

The development of vehicles continued as philhellenes described his strong reaction to Yokeup's comments, further escalating the story through juxtaposing elements of both the *Titanic* story and with images of burning. In philhellenes' next video entitled 'I Was Wrong' (V7), the new story complemented the *Titanic* metaphorical story, and more explicitly highlighted the Holocaust imagery that he initially claimed to have tried to avoid. philhellenes said:

> I think it comes from the image his video put in my head of field after field of endless piles of humans, the animal that suffers the most ... burning ... and that tiny little laugh that Yokeup let out ... he'd get into the lifeboat I'm sure. But if we were both actually witnessing those piles of so many burning people: atheists, agnostics, homosexuals, Muslims, Hindus, Sikhs, Buddhists, the Amish and the Jains ... And all the others that disagreed with the prophet Yokeup ... And that bastard was at my side ... And he let that tiny laugh out ... And I was armed ... It would be the last sound he ever made.

In this story, Yokeup and philhellenes are both surveying 'field after field' of burning bodies when Yokeup laughs. In addition to extending the metaphorical story to explicitly state his reaction to Yokeup, this version of the story further redeployed human garbage dumps to 'atheists, agnostics, homosexuals, Muslims, Hindus, Sikhs, Buddhists, the Amish, and the Jains, and all the others that disagreed with the prophet Yokeup'. philhellenes again retold the metaphorical story in the comments section of 'I Was Wrong' (V7), focusing on describing burning bodies and rejecting the initial story as seen. philhellenes wrote:

> Forget the lifeboat. It's a different scenario. I think you're inviting me to imagine my other scenario; endless fields of burning humans (practically all of humanity) as far as the eye could see, a sky black with the smoke, and yourself instead of Yokeup letting out a laugh. How would I react?
>
> Fascinating, thought provoking question. It feels different, certainly. Also feels different if I imagine JF777 laughing. I'd put it down to trauma in both cases. I don't feel anger in that scenario.

philhellenes began by stating, 'Forget the lifeboat.' Rather than continuing to explicate and extend the *Titanic* metaphorical story like other commenters, philhellenes posited a new story, one the video suggested he saw when he first heard Yokeup's video. Here again, philhellenes focused on Yokeup's lack of empathy and the moral question that emerged as a key element after responses by commenters to the initial story. The references to the *Titanic* are removed, but the trace of the metaphor remains in how the story is constructed, reflecting the initial action the story accomplished: voicing philhellenes' displeasure with Yokeup. The retelling of the stories, particularly the piles of 'so many burning people' changed the emphasis of the metaphorical story from a joke told about another user, to a focus on Yokeup's description of others burning, which philhellenes had originally found offensive. The development of metaphors, therefore, followed philhellenes' attempts to engage users in his reaction to Yokeup and emphasize what he believed to be offensive about the use of garbage dumps and piles in describing other users.

Users not only repeated and developed individual vehicles in response to philhellenes, but the user oakleywellington also told a subversive version of the parable of the vine and branches, producing the following new metaphorical story:

> ...And so I was cast into the pile of withered tree limbs, my friends leaves shaking with uncertainty, but I lay there unafraid and my fellow tree limbs did wonder how I was so confident up until God's fire did start to burn. And my friends did realize why my leaves stayed calm and true as did theirs when they saw the fire consume us and we felt nothing for God's fire cannot burn us, for God's fire cannot burn logic and truth and love for each other. We lay in tact in the fire against God's will.

Here, the parable of the vine and branches was retold with the main elements and actions of the parable preserved without redeployment. The parable was extended in time, however, and although the branches are thrown into a fire, they are not burned. Vehicle development occurs as the tree limbs are presented as having leaves that shake with fear. Although the branches are thrown into a pile to be burned, the fire is unable to burn them because of their 'logic and truth and love' for each other. oakleywellington, therefore, appropriates power from the moral authority of the story and subverts it by suggesting that those who Yokeup had said will ultimately be burned cannot be destroyed.

In the same way as the development of the *Titanic* vehicles seen above, oakleywellington's comment shows how all the vehicles in a metaphorical story can be developed and extended. The individual, constituent elements of the John 15 parable were manipulated and subverted to display oakleywellington's beliefs and opinions. All the elements of oakleywellington's new story convey meaning in comparison and contrast to the meaning of the parable and the development of the stories by philhellenes. The pain and suffering of the burning from philhellenes' story is contrasted with leaves staying calm. The cut-off branches of the John 15 parable lay intact. The construction of the new story becomes a contextualized re-voicing of the previous discourse, with a particular meaning at a particular time.

Reference to the *Titanic* story did not reappear in subsequent discussions of Yokeup, despite vehicles including burn and the Holocaust-related imagery re-emerging in subsequent videos. The metaphorical story was, therefore, temporarily stable in the two videos, by elements of discourse preceding it, but not enduring or becoming a long-term resource for users. The parable of the vine and the branches, by contrast, continued to be a source of discussion. Analysis of the trajectory of human garbage in the dataset shows that the response users had to Yokeup influenced how they developed the metaphorical language. When user response to Yokeup was oriented towards his use of the Bible, the responses focused on whether or not he maintained the meaning of the Biblical text. On the other hand, when user response oriented towards the action of the metaphor as an offensive categorization of others, the responses focused on negatively evaluating Yokeup and using metaphorical language to further creative negative descriptions of him. In both cases, however, drama developed and both responses resulted in disagreement among users over whether or not what Yokeup had done was 'right', either in the exegesis of the text or in his words and/or actions.

In addition to negatively evaluating Yokeup by calling him a 'psychopath', philhellenes' response also included metaphorical verbal threats. In the *Titanic* story, the conclusion implied that philhellenes would prefer Yokeup to be dead. However, philhellenes' threats towards Yokeup were hedged as hypothetical or metaphorical, rather than as actual physical threats on Yokeup's life, because philhellenes presented the story as hypothetical, saying, '. . . but if we were both actually witnessing those piles of so many burning people . . . and that bastard was at my side . . . and he let that tiny laugh out . . . and I was armed . . . it would be the last sound he ever made'.

philhellenes implies here that Yokeup's laugh would lead to killing Yokeup, but the situation in which he and Yokeup were watching 'piles of so many burning people' emphasizes the imaginary nature of his threats. Although the scenario was not explicitly a joke (as the *Titanic* story), philhellenes' use of the discourse marker 'if' at the beginning of the story as well as use of 'would' in describing the potential outcome marked the story as hypothetical. philhellenes made no suggestion that he actually intended to harm Yokeup physically. The threat of physical violence within a metaphorical story, therefore, allowed for hearers to interpret philhellenes' threat as non-violent while still asserting philhellenes' position of dominance over Yokeup.

Similar, hedged, hypothetical verbal threats directed at Yokeup were also present in responses to philhellenes' story, as seen in the following examples.

FarSideofTown wrote:

But after the initial reaction to his video, well, are you not right, about his version of the Christian doctrine, ... so if he truly thinks he is in some way trying to save souls, ... I mean, well, um, er, ... Oh Screw Him!

spleefrog9 commented:

I still hope a cartoon piano falls out of the sky and crushes him!
wow ... yokeup should die a miserable death.

And TheSuicidalOptimist wrote:

How can u watch his vids? I cannot as I find them so distasteful. According to YokeUp my loving, kind, generous parents (atheists and deceased) r now being tortured for eternity by his God. Now this alone would enrage me but for him to condone it is unforgivable. Any fundie espousing this to my face would be the recipiant of violence, sorry to say

Three strategies for making threats can be observed in the comments. In the first, FarSideofTown used a joke in the same way as philhellenes' *Titanic* story to present a violent action occurring to Yokeup, but the comedic nature of the comment made clear that the user was not presenting an intention to harm him. The next commenter wrote that Yokeup 'should die a miserable death', but did not suggest that the commenter would take violent action against Yokeup, rather that it would simply be good if it occurred. The final comment by TheSuicidalOptimist also created a hypothetical narrative in which, if TheSuicidalOptimist were to meet Yokeup, TheSuicidalOptimist would respond violently. Neither the commenters nor philhellenes' threats appeared to violate the basic community standards on YouTube since they were not specific nor worded to suggest actual physical violence.

Within the 'human garbage' drama, although no evidence of users intending to physically harm Yokeup was present, in the summer of 2009, Yokeup made several videos claiming to have been physically threatened and showing himself placing loaded handguns in his truck. Never in the video page corpus nor in my subsequent observation was any physical altercation reported. The displaying of handguns and Yokeup's pledges to protect himself and his wife also appeared to be attempts to counter offensive talk rather than suggest physical aggression towards others, and I saw no evidence in the video page corpus or observation period that Yokeup made verbal threats towards anyone. This suggests that the users intended for their words and threats to be understood within the context of the community in which users could not physically harm one another, but only encourage others to view them as dominant. The comments, however, did express the clear message about Yokeup that philhellenes had voiced in his video: that Yokeup's words had made him worthless and that he should be stopped.

philhellenes' attempt to dominate Yokeup did not go without challenge. Yokeup attempted to counter philhellenes by responding with his own categorization of philhellenes. Interaction between Yokeup and philhellenes occurred briefly in the comments section of 'YouTube's Psychopath: Yokeup.' (V5), where Yokeup sarcastically claims that philhellenes has done a good job editing, but says that God's truth 'will prevail'. Yokeup wrote:

> the searing truth got to ya . . . it always does and no matter how you edit what is said, the truth . . . to evil like you . . . will be haunting . . . Good job here. yep, my words, your editing. . . . but the truth will always prevail. You need Christ, and you know that.

philhellenes then responded by writing:

> Keep telling it as you see it, Jeff. Never stop. Pick up your efforts to a new level. You need to work harder. Make more videos like the one that got to me (which I admit DID get to me). Jesus is patting a cushion at his right side just for you.

philhellenes' verbal threat contained in the video was thwarted when Yokeup failed to be offended. Instead, Yokeup again presented his belief that other users were offended, not by his own use of 'garbage', but by the 'truth' of the Bible. Yokeup countered philhellenes, saying that philhellenes was unable to understand the truth because he was 'evil'. philhellenes' comment then attempted to thwart Yokeup by treating Yokeup in a condescending and sarcastic way and encouraging him to continue to 'tell it as you see it'. In both cases, the users presented themselves as not being offended, instead attributing their own meaning to the other's words.

This interaction between Yokeup and philhellenes also showed the difficulty of actually dominating another user on the site. Although contempt shown for Yokeup did not stop him from using 'human garbage', Yokeup's initial video containing the insult of Crosisborg was taken down, and Yokeup employed a new approach, using the Bible to support his categorization of others as 'garbage'. Crosisborg also removed his videos containing descriptions of Yokeup's wife Caroline after Yokeup expressed contempt for Crosisborg. Although Crosisborg continued to make drama videos about and directed at Yokeup, the change in actions towards Caroline showed that contempt may have affected how he subsequently behaved, although Crosisborg did not admit this. None of Yokeup's subsequent videos explicitly referenced Crosisborg and no more drama between the two individual users occurred in the video page corpus.

In the arguments between users, YOUTUBE ARGUMENT IS VIOLENT STRUGGLE emerged as a systematic metaphor. Although descriptions of arguments in terms of violence were observed, as with critique of war as a primary conceptual metaphor to describe contentious argument (Ritchie, 2003), the nature of the violent conflict was not clearly cast as a particular kind of struggle. Although vehicles from the WAR-MILITARY grouping were occasionally present in descriptions of arguments between users, particularly enemy, metaphors of violence were more often employed to describe aggressive action taken towards another. Users most frequently referred to arguments as attacking and defending. These vehicles not only described, but were arguments that included 'personal' attacks and criticism of another person.

The ambiguity of the violent struggle of YouTube drama could be seen in the following examples of attack describing YouTube drama videos. For example, Caroline, Yokeup's wife, used being attacked to describe the experience of arguing about Yokeup's videos. Although the topic for attack is not stated explicitly, from the preceding talk, attacking appeared to include insults and malicious criticism. This was also clear in the third extract in which attacking occurred on a personal level. Similarly, Christian user gdy80 attempted to make clear that his questioning of Yokeup and Caroline did not consist of attacking and asked them not to take it as such. Attacking could, therefore, also include non-malicious argumentation perceived as an insult; that is, users could attack others without necessarily having an intention to do so.

Surprisingly, the potential systematic metaphor ARGUMENTS BETWEEN USERS ON YOUTUBE IS DRAMA could not be constructed from the metaphors used in the dataset. Although the vehicle drama was present in the video page corpus, it only appeared four times. Users did not develop the vehicle to describe their interactions, and related metaphors either in terms of stories or theatre were not present. The labelling of the event as 'all the latest drama going on' by Yokeup suggests that 'drama' was an emic term used for the interaction in the video page corpus of the channel and not developed in interaction.

Responses to Yokeup did not always take an aggressive tone or imply physical domination. PaulsEgo, in the video entitled 'A Spotlight.' (V6), responded negatively to Yokeup and his actions, using humour rather than aggression. PaulsEgo reported that Yokeup actually made him happy because Yokeup was doing something PaulsEgo could not do in his 'position as an atheist' by 'shining a spotlight on everything that is dirty and depraved and disgusting and wrong about Christianity' and doing it 'from the inside'. In this description, Yokeup's words became thwarted because, rather than being offended, PaulsEgo interpreted Yokeup's actions as evidence that Christianity was bad. In this response, Yokeup's message was impeded through PaulsEgo's reinterpretation, and PaulsEgo attempted to dominate Yokeup, not by limiting his ability to speak freely, but taking away his ability to define the meaning of his words.

Humour continued to play a central role in PaulsEgo's response to Yokeup and in effecting a negative response to Yokeup in the comments. At the end of 'A Spotlight.' (V6), PaulsEgo voiced mock support for Yokeup, concluding the video by offering 'peace' to his viewers and 'a nice spoonful of piping hot hate grits with butter' to Yokeup. PaulsEgo implicitly devalued Yokeup in a similar way to Crosisborg by calling Yokeup 'white trash'. Although philhellenes' video implied a verbal threat of Yokeup in an apparent attempt to stop Yokeup from making videos, PaulsEgo encouraged Yokeup to continue to make videos. In philhellenes' approach, Yokeup's removal from YouTube would restrict Yokeup by making it impossible for him to interact with others on the site. In PaulsEgo's approach, perception of Yokeup as representative of Christianity would limit

Yokeup's ability for his message to be heard because what he said ultimately reflected negatively on him and Christianity. Although the tactic of the response was different, both videos suggested that restricting Yokeup's message from being heard as he desired and encouraging negative responses would result in less influence for Yokeup.

Attempts to restrict Yokeup's influence were not limited to non-Christian responses. christoferL, rather than calling Yokeup out by name as the others had done, presented an exegesis of the Bible that contrasted with Yokeup's. This allowed christoferL to avoid both directly disagreeing with Yokeup and clearly stating whether or not he viewed calling another user 'human garbage' negatively. Although christoferL did not explicitly mention Yokeup, the suggestion that Yokeup's exegesis was wrong did appear to attempt to limit Yokeup's influence on others. christoferL stated that in the justification for 'human garbage' using John 15, 'a rather obvious point has been ignored', suggesting that Yokeup had not read the parable carefully and his subsequent words and actions were, therefore, illegitimate. Christian commenters who responded to christoferL's video were also indirect and avoidance of using Yokeup's name can also be observed in comments such as: 'I'm sure I know who used the term "human garbage" and one thing he fails to remember is that Christ can redeem all'. Explicit presentation of Yokeup's use of 'garbage' as offensive was also avoided with users stating, 'humans are wonderfully and fearfully mad' and 'Bit of an oximoron "human garbage"'. The commenters used language that did not necessarily result in impoliteness, and an intention to cause offence was not presented. Instead, the Christian commenters wrote in a way similar to christoferL, suggesting that Yokeup was wrong without explicitly attempting to silence him.

During the observation period, some Christians did, however, like Crosisborg, philhellenes, and PaulsEgo directly and aggressively oppose Yokeup in comments and through response videos. These videos and comments publicly and explicitly rebuked him, but by the time of data collection, none of them were publicly available. Indeed, finding aggressive videos made by Christians proved to be difficult. One video made by the user PeaceInChristAlone in the summer of 2010, well after the initial drama, did name and receive a negative response from Yokeup, but otherwise, no evidence of strong opposition to 'human garbage' from Christians in videos remains online, suggesting a reluctance among some Christians to preserve drama videos.

Yokeup's explicit reporting of his intentions and reasons for his words and actions presented himself as attempting to follow his religious convictions and receive what he perceived to be the approval of God rather than that of other users. His discourse, however, suggested that he perceived influence over others, particularly other Christians in the community, as desirable since he repeatedly attempted to persuade them to agree with his exegesis. There was no explicit evidence, however, in the video page corpus that Yokeup was successful in convincing users to agree with him. This had the potential to occur, but given the limited nature of observation, attaining this information simply by analysing video pages seems unlikely. Still, the lack of evidence in the video corpus showed that, at least in the short term, his attempts to broaden his influence were not successful.

Although the word 'p'wning' (the emic, user term for dominating another user) was not regularly used in this drama, showing dominance over other users and, in particular, the search of the 'last word' (Billig, 1996) did contribute to the development of drama as users responded to offence in chains of attempts to dominate others. However, in the same way as Billig's theorization of argumentation (1996) shows that responses can lead to an endless answering of claims, response to others did not necessarily resolve arguments. Instead, users became caught up in answering one another. The responses did not always take the same form, and three different ways of attempting to respond to Yokeup have been identified. First, philhellenes and Crosisborg responded to Yokeup by explicitly undermining his message. Second, PaulsEgo thwarted Yokeup by responding to Yokeup with humour. And third, christoferL responded to Yokeup through use of scripture and challenging Yokeup's exegesis. These responses also attempted to dominate Yokeup and led to more drama when users disagreed over the appropriate response to Yokeup or when Yokeup himself responded.

Discussion

Throughout the 'human garbage' drama, the use of metaphorical stories as well as parables from the Bible showed evidence of Gibbs' notion of *allegoresis* (Gibbs, 2011:122). This occurred in the form of metaphorical stories told explicitly in discourse, but also implicitly in reference to metaphorical language from the Bible and references to the Holocaust which never appeared as complete stories. Both implicitly and explicitly, use of metaphorical stories and systematic metaphor in discourse about the present, immediate context was a process in which users drew on relevant socio-historical themes to talk about their own experiences. The themes that were relevant to the community emerged and shifted over time as different users interacted.

Metaphorical stories and metaphorical language, therefore, became a part of the community's knowledge that users engaged in once they were introduced into the discourse, often in creative ways, extending not only the stories, but the action embedded in the story. The stories moved in and out of prominence at different times. Users recognized metaphorical language that was specific to the community, in particular, the use of 'human garbage' and the metaphorical language taken from the Bible surrounding Yokeup's justification for its use, but this resource of metaphor was specific to the context and did not necessarily endure as a 'jargon' or 'ingroup/outgroup' language, a feature of internet 'community' that Herring (2004) has observed. Metaphors as a resource in the community were then temporary stabilities that endured on different timescales, depending on the interaction of users.

The symbolic themes to which users connected their own actions and the actions of others evidenced interconnecting systems of socially situated language use and cognitive activity, a key assumption of the discourse dynamics approach to metaphor (Cameron et al., 2009). When stories and systematic metaphor use emerged in discourse, users developed them in ways that revealed their own attitudes and beliefs, adapting and adjusting different elements in the course of interaction. The stories and themes did not, however, remain separate and were observed developing with inter-connected trajectories. The result of this inter-connection was evidenced in philhellenes' final story in which he and Yokeup have gone from standing on the deck of the *Titanic* to a generic space where they are looking at fields of burning bodies. In this instance, two otherwise unrelated historical stories, the Holocaust and the *Titanic*, became connected in a meaningful way because of unique discourse that proceeded it.

The development of metaphors from both parables and historical stories evidenced how metaphor from fixed, written texts or stable tragic historical narratives could take on new meaning as resources in local contexts of discourse where they can be adjusted and adapted. The result of this adaptation was not only new metaphors such as Yokeup is Hitler or unbelievers are human garbage which became meaningful in the particular community, but also systematic metaphors like CHRISTIAN BELIEF IS MENTAL ILLNESS. Like the stories, the individual systematic metaphors could be stable at different timescales, for a single video page, or across several video pages, or over a much longer period, depending on how they were used and reused. The parables and stories from which the metaphors were developed, however, remain fixed and accessible for new formulations in different contexts, enduring beyond and separate from their development in the community.

The relationship between the stories and systematic metaphor also supports a dynamic description of metaphor use, in which differentiating between 'systematic metaphor', 'metaphorical stories', 'scenarios', and 'parables' can be difficult when considering actual discourse. The development of the metaphorical stories could be empirically observed in metaphor shifting when users interpreted and developed the language to meet the particular context of the discourse, but stories could, at different times, be described as 'scenarios' or 'systematic metaphors' or Biblical metaphorical language, depending on the particular stretch of discourse being analysed. At any given point in the 'human garbage' drama and the development of metaphorical language, the discourse that preceded the individual use was essential to understanding why certain metaphors were being produced at certain times. The emerging context of discourse elucidated metaphorical language in a way that conceiving of 'scenarios' only as 'idealised cognitive models' (Lakoff, 1987) or setting up blended cognitive spaces (Crisp, 2008) might not. Because the metaphorical language was particular to the discourse context, describing the use in terms of fixed conceptual mappings or cognitive blends would likely be insufficient.

Analysis of metaphor also showed that within the community the enduring themes were often drawn from the Bible and users often spoke about the 'human garbage' drama metaphorically using language from the Bible. Although the users disagreed about how the parables should be interpreted, Christians did not disagree that the Bible *should* be used to describe the actions of others. The text of the Bible was a key resource in exegesis and users supported their readings of particular passages of the Bible by using other passages in the same way Bartkowski's (1996) research showed that Christians interpreted the contested passages in the Bible using other parts of the Bible. Because the authority was inherent in Biblical words and not in a fixed institutional reading, a Christian could claim, using evidence from other parts of the Bible, that their reading represented the true meaning.

The words of the Bible were also used to extend moral authority to a user's own words, similar to the 'second-order discourses' and 'pastoral power' in Foucault's (1981, 1982) description of the institutional church in which the words about the Bible appropriate and extend its authority. When Yokeup developed metaphor vehicles from the parable of the vine and the branches (John 15), claiming that the extension was all 'red ink' (or the exact words of Jesus), Yokeup implied that the words were authoritative because they were the words of the Bible and not simply his own. The right to speak in the way that he had was rooted in the words of the text. For users who recognized the authority of the Bible, Yokeup's words then also had the authority of the central text standing in for the institution of the church, provided that they would accept his exegesis.

The effective use of Biblical metaphorical language highlighted the role of metaphor in *pathos* in user arguments, a finding that supports Charteris-Blacks' (2009) work showing how metaphor is used in political discourse. For Christians, including Yokeup, christoferL, and commenters on their video pages, metaphorical language taken from the Bible was used often without qualification, evidencing its ubiquity as a shared reference among Christians from diverse backgrounds interacting on the site. By using Biblical metaphor, Christians could 'sound right' in their interaction with one another, drawing on a shared socio-religious context that they, despite their differences in exegesis of scripture, appeared to share. The use of Biblical metaphor helped them heighten the *pathos* of their argument because others both implicitly and explicitly might be expected to recognize their words as coming from the Bible.

Belief about the moral authority of the Bible also complicated drama because it appeared that Christians often spoke of and appealed to the Bible's authority without viewing it negatively, while atheists often appeared to have a negative view of the Bible. Yokeup's attempts to justify himself by appealing to the Bible's authority then only resulted in more impoliteness. Because atheists viewed the

Bible negatively, any use of the Bible, rather than diminish the negative views of others, only resulted in more impoliteness. Since Yokeup regularly appealed to the moral authority of the Bible, the language of the Bible was consistently a central topic of discussion and disagreement among all users.

The use of the Bible in arguments and appeals to exegesis indicated how 'enduring' socio-historical power resources contributed to each individual attempt at dominance and evidenced the same appeals to the authority of the Bible and the institutional church that have been used throughout history to exert control (Foucault, 1981). Exegesis by Yokeup and christoferL and the lack of appeals to denominational authorities also revealed the 'supremacy' of the Bible not only in Evangelical Christian theology (Packer, 1978), but in defining 'right' words and actions. The practice of exegesis to assert the authority of one's position showed that although Christians had shared beliefs, these beliefs did not necessarily lead to agreement, a finding that supports Bartkowski's (1996) observation that 'literal' readings of the Bible can still result in disagreement among Christians.

Differences in beliefs and conceptions of faith also had implications for perceptions of dominance, and who had or did not have power depended on the user's conception of positive face. Having a large number of subscribers and views appeared to be one measure of perceived power since it allowed users to spread their message. In this instance, power was equated with influence. For the Christians, however, although a positive value was placed on influence, a higher value appeared to be placed on the perception that their words were sanctioned by God and the Bible. Although influence was something that Christians like Yokeup and christoferL evidently sought, when it was seen as conflicting with piety, they evaluated it negatively.

The differences in expectations about social interaction were made most clear in the welcoming position Yokeup took towards 'hate'. Confounding a simple notion of positive and negative face (Brown & Levinson, 1987) or even a more nuanced understanding of face as culturally specific (O'Driscoll, 1996), Yokeup's stated proud acceptance of 'hate' from others, including both Christians and non-Christians, showed how negative evaluation from others could be desired and sought out, in the same way that internet 'trolls' seek negative attention (Hardaker, 2010). Yokeup's desire for negative reaction, however, was rooted in a belief about God from the Bible. His response to others' negative reactions highlights how different beliefs can lead to different outcomes and continue to generate drama. Because receiving negative attention for acting in a way that was perceived as affiliated with God resulted in positive face and a dominant position for Yokeup, he continued to pursue negative attention. This position, however, was also complex because other Christians made a distinction between impoliteness resulting when one had acted in accordance with the Bible and impoliteness resulting when one had acted in a negative way that was not justified by the Bible. Among Christians, drama developed around this disagreement, and user interaction revealed differences in how users believed they should respond to impoliteness, stemming from Christian belief.

Because the metaphorical language often included negative evaluations of others, the extension and development of metaphor also often repeated the negative evaluation. In this way, drama developed when metaphor shifting was tied to the mistreatment of another user or category of user, both in Yokeup's development of 'human garbage' to describe everyone he did not view as a 'believer' and in other people's offensive language about Yokeup. In both cases, whenever the development of this negative metaphorical language occurred, it prolonged drama by giving users new ways to negatively evaluate others. Metaphor was also used to escalate negative evaluations of others, using hyperbolic, exaggerated metaphorical language related to an initial metaphorical description of another. This was particularly important in the categorizations of Yokeup, when, for example, philhellenes' categorization of him as a psychopath was developed to the extreme, eventually comparing Yokeup with Hitler. In this way, the creative use of metaphor in the 'human garbage' drama interaction tended towards exaggeration and hyperbole as users developed descriptions of Yokeup.

Description and analysis of metaphor using metaphor-led discourse analysis has elucidated how users employed both metaphorical stories and systematic metaphors in discourse about social interaction to display their 'ideas, attitudes, and values' (Cameron et al., 2010:128). Analysis of metaphor has also shown the action of this metaphor use, that users employed metaphor to not only describe their social interaction, but also to effect change in the community, presenting others and their actions in a negative way and using metaphor to present themselves and their own actions in a positive way.

4

Fake Christians and Fluffy Christians: Metaphor in the Categorization of Users

In the initial series of insults among Crosisborg, Yokeup, and philhellenes, what a person was – 'human garbage' or a 'psychopath' or a 'good' Christian – became a central part of the disagreement. The recurring categorization of people in the drama as different categories of 'Christian' (e.g. 'good Christians' and 'bad Christians') grew out of this, often drawing on Biblically derived (metaphorical) categories, such as 'saved'. In this chapter, I will look specifically at the use of categories in the drama, particularly the relationship between metaphor and categorization, but I will also show how the use of the category of 'Christian' by many different people, often involved conflicting descriptions of the same category depending on the position of the user employing the category. I will show how categories did more than simply allow users to group and affiliate, but instead provided a way to attack and belittle others.

Membership categorization analysis

Prior to the interest in social categorization in the twentieth century and analysis of categorization in conversation, understanding of categories was dominated by the classical view, developed by Plato and Aristotle, which held that categories had clear boundaries defined by common properties and were uniform in respect to centrality (i.e. no members of the category were more representative of the category than others) (Lakoff, 1987). In this view of categorization, no member of the category has any special status as all category members are united only by shared attributes. Although this view of categorization was not, as Lakoff (1987) points out, built on empirical research into categorization in thought or interaction, pragmatically it is largely sufficient for speakers in day-to-day interaction. Instances when categories are challenged and the process of categorization is explicitly at issue, however, require a more nuanced description of categorization phenomena, particularly as they relate to social organization and interaction.

In the twentieth century, this classical view of categorization was challenged, beginning with the work of Wittgenstein (1953) who suggested that categorization may not be based on common attributes, but rather on family resemblance between members of a category, that is, member traits that were similar. Wittgenstein used the example of the category 'games', showing that though there is no common attribute between all games, they are, like family members, similar to one another in a wide variety of ways. Wittgenstein also suggested that categories can have central and non-central members, and that there are good and bad examples of a category, members that are more typical of a category than others. Wittgenstein's work, however, did not focus exclusively on social categorization and was not based on empirical evidence of categorization in talk or cognition.

Key research in the field of cognitive science challenged common-sense understandings of categorization with empirical data. Rosch's (1973, 1978) prototype theory of categorization takes the notion of central and non-central category members further, suggesting that within categories, prototypical members can be found. Drawing on the notion of 'cognitive economy', in which humans attempt to get the most amount of information from a category with the least amount of cognitive effort, Rosch describes a 'prototype' as the clearest case of 'category membership defined operationally by people's judgements of goodness of membership in the category' (1973:36), and this notion of prototypicality has been observed in studies of colour prototypes (Rosch, 1974, 1975). Importantly, in line with later work by Gibson (1979), Rosch suggested that, for some categories, rather than arbitrary combinations of features that comprise a category, cultures and individuals discover correlations and build categories based on the correlations (Markman, 1991).

Following from this research, interest in categorization emerged in sociology, particularly in social identity theory, which is closely tied to the theory of self-categorization (Hornsey, 2008; Turner, 1985; Turner & Hogg, 1987). In the social identity theory framework, Tajfel viewed categories as closely related to group membership and self-identity (Tajfel, 1977) and argued that 'the content of the categories to which people are assigned by virtue of their social identity is generated over a long period of time within a culture' (Tajfel, 1981:134). The basis of categorization then is the individual's flexible view of themselves as 'I', those they are related to in a group as 'we', and those outside of their ingroup as 'them' (Tajfel & Turner, 1986), with different social categories being emphasized at different times, given situational pressures (Ray, Mackie, Rydell, & Smith, 2008).

Although ostensibly a new theory attempting to refine and elaborate on the cognitive elements of social identity theory, social categorization theory shares much of the same assumptions about intergroup relations and identity with social identity theory (Hornsey, 2008). Self-categorization theory (Turner & Hogg, 1987) '[specifies] the operation of the social categorization process as the cognitive basis of group behaviour. Social categorization of self and others into ingroup and outgroup accentuates the perceived similarity of the target to the relevant ingroup or outgroup prototype (cognitive representation of features that describe and prescribe attributes of the group)' (Hogg & Terry, 2000:123). Like Rosch's approach, self-categorization theory treats prototypes not as 'checklists of attributes but, rather, fuzzy sets that capture the context-dependent features of group membership' (Hogg & Terry, 2000:123; Zadech, 1965). Like Rosch's notion of categories as culturally and individually dependent, context plays an important role in self-categorization theory in how an individual categorizes him or herself and others at any given time, but the categories map onto social groups deriving from a speaker's own understanding of her or his identity in relation to others.

Group and self-identity remains central in social theory about social categorization. The category, in this sense, is a name for a group, and in the case of ethnicity, a proper name. Tajfel's work argued that ingroup bias leads to intergroup discrimination (Tajfel, 1970), a view that has remained dominant in research into intergroup discrimination and impoliteness (see Bodenhausen, Mussweiler, Gabriel, & Moreno, 2001; Nelson, 2009; Ray et al., 2008). Categorization can then serve that purpose of accentuating how individuals in groups view themselves as different from individuals in outgroups. Turner and others (Abrams & Hogg, 2010; Turner, 1981), for example, have argued that categorization can lead to stereotyping and depersonalization, based on focusing on several alleged shared characteristics in groups and ignoring diversity within groups (Wetherell, 1996). Categorizations, however, and stereotypes that arise from salient categories are not, Turner argued, fixed mental representations, but contextual, depending on which category and group an individual is comparing themselves to (Haslam & Turner, 1992; Hornsey, 2008).

The categorization in the drama that we have so far investigated, however, shows a use of categories that is particularly context dependent. The category 'human garbage' for example, which Yokeup applied to users in the drama, was not a labelling of a particular group of people, but instead a category that he applied in specific stretches of discourse to accomplish particular actions, like insulting other users. The categories did not serve as labels for groups so much as descriptions of individuals at particular moments. Like metaphor, those categories could be adopted and adapted by others, or they could be appropriated, subverted, or developed, depending on the context of interaction and whom a speaker was addressing.

In contrast to approaches to categorization as a function of labelling group and self-identity and cognitive approaches focusing on the processes of categorization in the mind, membership categorization analysis focuses on the local use of categories in interaction between speakers. Membership categorization analysis has developed from the conversation analyst Sacks' early lectures on analysis of calls made to suicide-prevention lines in the 1960s (Sacks, 1995). Drawing on Goffman's (1967) ethnomethodology, Sacks stressed that membership categories were not necessarily labels for social groups (Sacks, 1995), but rather that membership categorization comprised the 'procedures people employ to make sense of other people and their activities' (Leudar, Marsland, & Nekvapil, 2004:244) and describes the process by which people use everyday knowledge to categorize the world around them in conversation (Lepper, 2000; Sacks, 1995).

Sacks, and subsequent work by Schegloff (1972), Drew (1978), and Jayussi (1984), focused on describing and analysing acts of membership categorization in talk, developing means to identify and describe how speakers did the work of categorization.

Sacks used the following example taken from a child's story to describe the process of categorization: 'The baby cried. The mommy picked it up'. From the story, Sacks argued, listeners were able to infer the relationship between the mother and child using rules of membership in categories and membership categorization devices, or 'collection[s] of categories plus rules of application' (Lepper, 2000:17). In the example, Sacks argued the hearer understands the two categories ('mommy' and 'baby') in terms of the collection of 'family' and the category-bound activity of 'picking up'. Membership categorization devices provide the guide for placing members into categories and provide an accounting for the expectancies people take for granted when categorizing others (Eglin & Hester, 2003).

Membership categorization analysis process focuses on the process of categorization in talk. Membership categories are 'classifications or social types that might be used to describe persons' (Hester & Eglin, 1997:3), but membership categories can also describe any way of grouping together people, actions, or locations (Drew, 1978; Schegloff, 2007). Membership categories can be grouped together into collections of related categories, such as the categories of 'mommy' and 'baby' comprising the collection of 'family' above, and can be explicitly stated in talk, or inferred from the context. Category-bound activities are the actions that apply to the members of a certain category and tell the kinds of things that members of a certain membership category do. Watson (1978) subsequently extended the notion of category-bound activities to category-bound predicates, including not only what a member of a certain category does, but any other characteristics of a category.

Sacks (1995) argued there were two key rules for categorization: consistency and economy. The consistency rule requires that when a category from a collection is applied to one member of the population, the same category or another category from the collection applies to all members; that is, if a membership categorization device is used to categorize one member of a category, the membership categorization device must also apply to all other members of the category. The economy rule is described by Schegloff as:

> When some category from some collection of categories in a membership categorization device has been used to refer to (or identify or apperceive) some person on some occasion, then other persons in the setting may be referred to or identified or apperceived or grasped by reference to the same or other categories from the same collection.
>
> (Schegloff, 2007:471)

In this case, even if a membership categorization device is not explicitly applied to a category member, the membership categorization device applied to one member may be applied to any other category members, a concept later challenged in the reconsidered model of membership categorization analysis proposed by Housley and Fitzgerald (2002). Lepper (2000) also points out that from Sacks' example of the mommy and the baby, the linking of members in standardized relational pairs can also be present as a rule for applying a membership categorization device and that pairings of members in standardized relational pairs bring expectations and obligations for the members in relationship to one another.

Two additional key elements of membership categories are that they are 'inference-rich' – that is, they store societal knowledge about the particular category; and that they are 'representative' – that is, 'any member of any category is a representative of that category of the purpose of use of whatever knowledge is stored about that category' (Sacks, 1995:41). The knowledge stored about the category, however, may differ depending on the societal knowledge that speakers and hearers hold. For example, the category of 'Christian' will reflect different stored knowledge depending on the person. Rather than consider 'prototypes' for categories as Rosch proposed, the representative nature of Sacks' description of categories suggests that anyone, once categorized, represents the category they occupy and their actions as typical of that category. Sacks' 'viewer's maxim' also describes this as: 'If a member sees a category-bound activity being done, then, if one can see it being done by a member of a category to which the activity is bound, then: See it that way' (Sacks, 1974:225).

In recent applications of membership categorization analysis, the key concepts of membership categorization analysis have been applied to analysis of contextual categorization. Housley and Fitzgerald note that:

> [U]tterances often not only derive their sense from 'stocks of common sense knowledge' but can also, in terms of categories in context, be mapped and tied to other categories in terms of locally situated conditions of relevance, activity and context.
>
> (Housley and Fitzgerald, 2002:68)

Housley and Fitzgerald suggest, then, a model of membership characterization analysis which emphasizes the contextual interaction and resources of individuals and can be used to elucidate the mechanisms of categorization in discourse (Fitzgerald & Housley, 2007; Housley & Fitzgerald, 2009). Membership categories are not analysed as pre-existing with accepted referents, but rather 'membership categorization devices or collections are ... regarded as *in situ* achievements of members' practical actions and practical reasoning' (Hester, 1994:242 cited in Housley and Fitzgerald, 2002) and contingent on the knowledge and experiences of the others in the context. Categorization is analysed as a contextual phenomenon. They are not common-sense 'stocks of knowledge' dictating the use of categories. Instead, repeated uses of categories by speakers in situated contexts also influence how common-sense knowledge about categories emerges over time.

Employing membership categorization analysis in an attempt to analyse categorization in context, Eglin and Hester investigate the contextual use of the category of 'feminist' in the Montreal Massacre (2002), and work by Evaldsson (2005) employs membership categorization analysis coupled with observations of insult (pejorative comments about a person's actions, possessions, or appearance) in groups of multi-ethnic children. Evaldsson (2007), as well as work by Jayyusi (1984) and later work by Fitzgerald and colleagues (Fitzgerald, 2012; Fitzgerald & Housley, 2007), has also shown that categories are tied to moral ordering, with categories used to link to value judgements about individuals to certain categories. These value judgements were, however, embedded in the context in which the categorization occurred, rather than in common-sense understandings of pre-established membership categories.

Doing categorization analysis

Building on Housley and Fitzgerald's work, I adapted the key analytic concepts of membership categorization analysis to analyse the contextual categorization of users within the three drama exchanges contained in the larger video corpus taking into account the sequential development of drama. I first described the individual, constituent elements of categorization, including category-bound activities and predicates, potential collections of categories, and implicit and explicit (standardized) relational pairs, in all the elements of the video page transcripts. I identified category-bound activities as actions linking subjects and objects, and category-bound predicates as any other characteristics of a category that did not necessarily involve actions. Potential collections (such as 'types of Christians') and relational pairs of categories (such as 'religious' and 'saved') were also identified as two or more categories that were related in the discourse, either through adjacency or semantic meaning.

To describe the sequential development of categories in user talk, I also noted where category-bound activities were shared among more than one category and how users employed them in different ways over time. Next, the development of the individual components of categorization on the video page was identified and shifts in uses recorded. I then constructed potential categorization devices where categories were used, and noted how different users employed the same or similar categories within different devices. Finally, to answer the research questions and aims, I looked in more detail at examples on categorization devices which were either the main topics of videos and/or disputed or developed by commenters and in video responses to investigate the role of categorization in the development of drama.

Although explicit categorization with explicit reference to category-bound activities was present in text or talk, in many cases (particularly in very short comments), the category-bound activities which linked the subjects to the objects were implicit. For example, in the comment 'Yokeup is a sick twisted asshole', no category-bound activities or predicates were present in the comment and the user did not post any more comments on the page. Where category-bound activities were not explicitly stated, following work by Eglin and Hester (2003) that investigated the construction of the category of 'feminist' in the context of discourse about a single event (the Montreal Massacre), I looked for the same categories ('sick' and 'asshole') with explicit category-bound activities at other places on the video page. In this case, the commenter repeated two categories from the video talk in which philhellenes described Yokeup as 'sick' and an 'asshole'. The category-bound activities in philhellenes' talk, namely, 'speaking in a hateful way' and 'using the Bible to justify bad behaviour', could therefore potentially be used to elucidate the meaning of the commenter's categorization.

In my analysis, I will employ in particular the concepts of 'category-bound activities and predicates' and 'membership categorization devices' in analysing how users categorized one another and how disagreements between users developed. As we have already seen, metaphorical categories played an important role in how users described one another and were often a source of disagreement among users.

Metaphorical categories and category-bound activities

As I showed in the analysis in the preceding chapter, metaphorical descriptions of Yokeup were repeatedly used, particularly in negative responses to his use of 'human garbage'. Central to the development of drama was not only Yokeup's categorization of others as 'human garbage', but the categorizations of Yokeup that developed in response, seen most vividly in the video entitled 'YouTube's Psychopath: Yokeup.' (V5), in which philhellenes called Yokeup a 'psychopath'. This insulting categorization was predicated on philhellenes' strong, visceral reaction to Yokeup's videos, which philhellenes stated in his video:

> You're kinda like a rabid dog. You've gone sick and with that type of sickness, I'm not sure there is a cure...When you're a psychopath, as you are, Jeff [Yokeup] ... And not all psychopath's have to do killing. It's a state of mind a complete lack of empathy with other human beings and I've never heard anyone ... I've never heard anyone talk with such a lack of empathy for their fellow humans.

philhellenes' response to Yokeup completely ignored Yokeup's appeal to the Bible as a means for justifying calling others 'human garbage'. Instead, philhellenes attacked Yokeup with the strongest possible language, comparing Yokeup to a rabid dog that has gone sick. In the climax of the video, philhellenes calls Yokeup a 'psychopath' based on two elements: an assertion of the category-bound activity of 'having a complete lack of empathy' and a rejection of a category-bound activity of 'doing killing'. Yokeup calling others 'garbage' was therefore used as a category-bound activity of 'psychopath' because it showed Yokeup's lack of empathy for other people. The use of the term was, however, ambiguous in that it was never clear whether or not philhellenes intended for the categorization to be heard literally or metaphorically.

philhellenes' strong rebuke of Yokeup served as an escalating move in the drama, taking Yokeup's own words and re-voicing them to show Yokeup in the worst possible light. The response did not take into account any of Yokeup's hedging around the use of the term and used his implication that the words were from the Bible not as a means to justify what Yokeup had said, but as further evidence of Yokeup's madness: his belief that what he was doing was sanctioned by God and acceptable in his understanding of God and religious practice. Yokeup was sick because he believed that God was supporting him.

The categorization seemed to imply Yokeup might also be a dangerous person. Although philhellenes explicitly rejected 'doing killing' as an activity for 'psychopaths', comments implied that Yokeup may be capable of violence. SecularNATION wrote, 'Sociopath suffering from christ-psychosis is a lethal combination', while another compared Yokeup with the serial killer John Wayne Gacy. Two more commenters wrote Yokeup was capable of violence and was sadistic, suggesting the category of 'psychopath' included an inference of violent action, despite philhellenes' explicit statement that it did not. In these responses, because 'psychopaths' are violent and Yokeup's words proved he was a 'psychopath', Yokeup was also capable of violence. Although philhellenes' use of metaphorical stories suggested that he was only comparing Yokeup to a 'psychopath' to emphasize Yokeup's lack of empathy, the response by commenters extended the categorization and escalated the negative evaluation by suggesting that Yokeup could also hurt others physically.

Support from the commenters further indicated the differences in reception to 'human garbage' between Christians and non-Christians. Only one commenter made mention of Yokeup's exegesis of the parable, but instead, users developed philhellenes' mental illness descriptions of Yokeup and extended descriptions of 'burning' to discourse about the Holocaust, particularly in descriptions of Yokeup as 'Hitler'. For these users, the discussion of the importance of the Bible in the development of the vehicle did not occur, but rather they developed philhellenes' hyperbolic language, further escalating and exaggerating his negative evaluations of Yokeup. philhellenes' use of the metaphor Yokeup is a psychopath resulted in the development of mental illness metaphors by users who evaluated Yokeup with language similar to philhellenes. Of the 613 comments on the video, 70 comments used metaphors related to mental illness. Users repeated the vehicle 'psychopath' and developed the vehicles to include 'batshit insane', 'deranged', and a 'lunatic', among others, emphasizing a negative evaluation of Yokeup's actions as unacceptable for mentally healthy individuals.

Insults of Yokeup also included metaphors related to mental illness. The verbal metaphor Yokeup is a psychopath was used in philhellenes' video entitled 'YouTube's Psychopath: Yokeup.', and throughout the course of his video, philhellenes explicated the meaning of psychopath, using literal, medical descriptions of psychopathy to describe Yokeup and Yokeup's actions. Commenters then further employed mental illness metaphors in categorizations of Yokeup both in short, one-line insults such as 'Yokeup is insane', as well as development of mental illness metaphors in descriptions of Yokeup's concrete actions. Further investigation of the topics of mental illness metaphors suggested that mental illness was used to negatively evaluate not only Yokeup's character and actions, but also Yokeup's reported belief that God approved of what he said. Through vehicle redeployment, mental illness descriptions of Yokeup were then applied to all Christians, constructing a systematic metaphor CHRISTIAN BELIEF IS MENTAL ILLNESS.

Although philhellenes made numerous negative evaluations and descriptions of Yokeup, when describing him particularly as a psychopath, philhellenes employed the metaphor 'you're a psychopath' in reference to 'Jeff', Yokeup's given name. In his explication of the metaphor, philhellenes followed a pattern of redeploying mental illness descriptions of Yokeup to all Christians. Although philhellenes negatively evaluated Yokeup's words as 'filth that comes out of your mouth', he also highlighted Yokeup's perceived spiritual experience as 'feel(ing) the love of God'. This description of spiritual experience was then presented as a 'problem' for 'all Christians', a problem that philhellenes said reinforced bias and created irrational anger. In the development of the 'psychopath' vehicle and philhellenes' description later in the video of Yokeup's insanity, mental illness vehicles were implicitly redeployed to all Christians. Yokeup's 'insanity' and his beliefs were presented as prototypical of Christians, similar to Dawkins' (2006) description of religious belief as 'delusion'.

A similar description of Yokeup's reports of his beliefs and motivations is present in the video entitled 'Yokeup: Poster Boy For Bad Christians' (V3). In this video, Crosisborg followed a similar narrative pattern, comparing Yokeup's actions, beliefs, and character with 'Christianity' more generally, saying: 'He also alluded to the fact that he's a prophet because he made numerous statements about how God speaks through him. That is a clear sign of insanity.' As in philhellenes' video, Crosisborg presented Yokeup's purported descriptions of spiritual experience and true belief. Up to this point in the video, Crosisborg had insulted Yokeup's intelligence and his social status, but in this description of Yokeup's belief, Crosisborg negatively evaluated it as 'a clear sign of insanity'. Yokeup's faith, therefore, led to an evaluation of Yokeup as insane. Through vehicle redeployment, mental illness vehicles were then extended to not only individual users, but the categories they occupied, creating a description of not only Yokeup, but Christian faith more generally. This happened explicitly in philhellenes' video, extracted above, and implicitly in Crosisborg's video as he described Yokeup's character as representative of what was wrong with 'Christianity'.

Finally, examples of commenters following the same pattern of conflating Yokeup's actions with those of Christians in general were also observed. BreadWinner06 wrote:

no you're wrong *hes a* poster child for Christianity (hes a real christian)

Howtofoldsoup commented:

I believe it was best worded as such: Good men tend to do good. Evil men tend to do evil. For a good man to do evil – that takes religion.

And Cootabux wrote:

I think label psychopath is too light. . .but your commentary in the video makes up for it!
Oh yes, he's keeping right in line with the true "spirit" of christian dogma! He would've been right at home had he been alive during the early church period.

In these comments, users responded to Crosisborg's claim that Yokeup was the 'poster boy for bad Christianity', which Crosisborg stated at the beginning of the video and which served as the video's title. In all three comments, users followed the same pattern as in philhellenes' and Crosisborg's videos: the evaluation of Yokeup as a psychopath was repeated and Yokeup's actions and traits were extended as descriptions of Christians in general, Christian belief, and God. The first comment in particular highlighted that Yokeup was insane because he behaved maliciously out of true belief. Although other insults of Yokeup as stupid or an asshole evaluated his actions as offensive, the comments did not link the insult to Yokeup's presentation of himself as acting out of true belief.

Yokeup's offensive words and actions coupled with his apparent sincere belief afforded users an opportunity to present Christian belief and practice negatively, encapsulated in the systematic metaphor CHRISTIAN BELIEF IS MENTAL ILLNESS. This systematic metaphor can be constructed from discourse on atheist video pages, but, unsurprisingly, did not appear on Christian video pages in discourse about belief. This showed that within the community, different users could employ different systematic ways of talking about the world. Here, the values and attitudes of the users employing the systematic metaphor were displayed because the metaphor included an obvious negative evaluation. Users who held a negative view of Christianity employed the metaphor, while users who were Christians or held positive views of Christianity did not.

Contrasted with this systematic metaphor, however, was metaphor use about spiritual experience, which produced the systematic metaphor GOD SPEAKS TO CHRISTIANS. The systematic metaphor appears to be derived from the Bible (e.g. Exodus 19.19, Job 37.5, Hebrews 4.7) and was used primarily on Christian video pages to talk about spiritual experience and belief. On Yokeup and christoferL's video pages, the ability to hear the voice of God was spoken of as unique to Christians and represented a privileged spiritual position. Yokeup said at one point, 'We don't listen to people. We listen to God. We listen to what God has to say.' Yokeup then performed an approach to the community that was not at least explicitly in the opinion of others, but rather focused on his own beliefs about the rightness and wrongness of what he should do. For Yokeup, 'listening to God' was far more important than being liked.

In contrast to other descriptions that linked hearing God's voice to mental illness and concrete instances of 'bad behaviour', this systematic metaphor was constructed from talk about spiritual experience that was not linked to concrete actions or events. For example, when asked by a user in the comments section of the video titled 'irrelevant' (V10) to further explain the process of hearing God's voice, Yokeup responded in the comments: 'well, if you don't believe in God, if you don't have a relationship, you won't understand. Ask any born-again believer and they will know exactly what it means to hear from God'. As Yokeup described, 'We listen to what God tells us and as believers, sold-out to Christ, his voice is clear to us'. In these comments, Yokeup presented his spiritual experience in terms of verbal communication: Yokeup, as believer, listened, and God spoke to him. The voice of God, in this metaphorical representation, was also clear, and the experience of hearing God's voice was described in certain and exact terms. Moreover, this belief did not appear to be unique to Yokeup and similar Biblical narratives can be found (e.g. Romans 10.17).

Communicating with God was, therefore, not limited to a single religious practice such as reading the Bible or praying, but was used to describe spiritual experience more generally. Whether or not a Christian heard God's voice through the speaking of another (as in preaching), from individual religious practice (as in prayer), or in reading the Bible, in the video page corpus all are described as God's word. Although the reading of the Bible appeared to be the most effective way for God to communicate with Christians, Christian religious practice or spiritual experience in the community was consistently spoken about in terms of speaking and hearing. Moreover, God was presented as using Christians to communicate with others. For example, a commenter praised Christian user JeromeStein4U writing, 'I see God speaking through you lately, brother'. This commenter, like Yokeup, referred to God as speaking and themselves as being able to see this speaking, using mixed perception metaphors to describe their spiritual experience.

The speaking of God was also used in discourse about the Bible where the Bible was presented as saying something or as the words of God. As in research into Evangelical Christian faith communities by Malley (2004), a relationship between the Biblical text and personal experience could be observed in the 'human garbage' drama as users supported their own thoughts and arguments while using the Bible. Although non-Christians questioned Yokeup's descriptions of his spiritual experience as communicating with God, the metaphor did not become an object of disagreement on Christian video pages, and christoferL and Yokeup were praised for speaking God's word and encouraged to listen to God. When disagreement about what God says occurred, users argued about Biblical interpretation rather than challenge the reporting of spiritual experience as in christoferL's video entitled 'John 15 for Dummies – Unbelievers are human garbage?' (V12) and Yokeup's video entitled 'more on. . .human garbage' (V14).

The metaphorical description of spiritual experience as communicating with God did appear to allude to the Bible, but a specific passage or quotation was never cited in the video page corpus. Yokeup, christoferL, and commenters on their video pages did not explicate stories of Biblical characters hearing the voice of God and no Biblical examples of a hearing God's voice metaphor could be observed in the corpus. The presence of the metaphor in the Biblical text in both the Old and New Testaments (see Proverbs 20.12, Isaiah 30.21, John 10.3, Hebrews 3.7) suggested it is a key framing device for speaking about spiritual experience in Christian belief, particularly because only abstract language exists for describing it. Given, however, that the metaphor was derived from the Bible, the development of speaking-hearing language in user talk away from the Bible and into descriptions of mental illness highlighted how an individual's beliefs influenced which metaphors users employed. For many of the atheists and non-Christians, hearing God was associated with a negative evaluation, but for Christians, it was associated with a positive evaluation.

Yokeup never made a video in response to philhellenes' claim or explicitly responding to the claim that he was a psychopath. Instead, Yokeup continued to use and repeat the categorization of others as 'garbage'. After its initial use and Yokeup's initial defence in response to others, the development of garbage from the parable of the vine and branches stabilized in the same form that Yokeup had used it in the video entitled 'more on...human garbage' (V14). Yokeup continued to argue that because the Biblical description of anyone who does not remain in [Christ] included contemporary readers of the text, and because garbage was thrown away in the same way that withered branches are thrown away, garbage was an acceptable development of withered branches. Subsequently, the metaphor anyone who does not remain in [Christ] is garbage was not only acceptable, but the word of God taken directly from the Bible.

The different treatment of the Bible among users resulted in further drama by exposing differences in expectations and beliefs about social interaction when users argued about each other's words or actions. For Yokeup and christoferL, reading aloud from and citing the Bible showed that their claims were authoritative and that what they said was supported by the 'word of God'. Non-Christians, however, treated the inclusion of offensive language from the Bible as further evidence that the Bible could be used to make Christians act like 'psychopaths' and show a lack of empathy for others.

This escalation continued in further commenter responses, which described Yokeup as being like 'Hitler', a prototypical 'Nazi' and developed philhellenes' statement that he would 'put piles of corpses as found in the concentration camps on the screen while you talked about human garbage dumps'.

philhellenes emphasized Yokeup's use of 'human garbage dumps' with descriptions of burning bodies, particularly relating it to the Holocaust, a powerful image that he returned to several times in the comments and the subsequent video in describing Yokeup's 'human garbage dumps'. Commenters then used the action of 'burning human garbage dumps' to describe Yokeup as acting like 'Hitler'. A commenter wrote, 'It was only a matter of time until the little square moustache popped out under his nose', using a reference to Hitler's iconic moustache to draw a comparison between the two. This comparison was repeated throughout the comments section, and in subsequent descriptions of Yokeup's 'calling others human garbage' was repeatedly used to compare Yokeup to 'Hitler'. Comparing other users to Hitler in online arguments is not by any means a new phenomenon, as Godwin describes: 'As an online discussion grows longer, the probability of a comparison involving Nazis or Hitler approaches one' (Godwin, 1994). The YouTube community investigated here appeared to be no exception to the resource of Hitler as a rhetorical device, and Yokeup's use of 'burning human garbage' allowed for an easy comparison that others quickly picked up on and developed.

Not all categorizations of Yokeup, however, drew comparisons between him and violent or mentally ill individuals. In the video titled 'Yokeup: Poster Boy For Bad Christians' (V3), Crosisborg categorized Yokeup as 'American white trash' without reference to any of Yokeup's particular words or actions. Crosisborg stated in the comments section of the video that he categorized Yokeup this way because 'trash' was a bad thing and he viewed Yokeup as bad. 'White trash' appeared to be a response to Yokeup's use of 'garbage', but although the 'trash' and 'garbage' are semantically similar, 'white trash' is also a conventionalized metaphorical category used to describe the rural poor, particularly in the US South (Wray & Newitz, 1997). The use of the category implied that Crosisborg negatively evaluated not only Yokeup's words and actions, but also his socio-regional position, further stereotyping him as racially and economically inferior to others (Wray & Newitz, 1997).

Yokeup's socio-cultural identity was often an unspoken issue in disagreements involving him in the community. In particular, the disagreement with Pastor Javid, which served as a starting point for the human garbage drama, appeared to have a racial element, with Pastor Javid at one time posting a video from the TV mini-series 'Roots' of a slave being whipped and suggesting that this was analogous to his experience on YouTube. Yokeup, however, in the corpus I gathered and in the videos I observed never made any negative comments related to Pastor Javid's race and did not address issues of race in his videos, beyond taking pride in his working-class persona and being from the South.

Commenters made inferences about the category 'American white trash' and described Yokeup as a racist in escalating negative evaluations. Examples of this escalation can be seen in these comments. theenforcer1977 wrote,

> Yokeup is racist, arrogant, violent and an egomaniac.

While Francie32 commented:

> People must flag his videos, he is not safe for America, he is a militant Nazi, I stand by my comments, that I trust you and Tommy way more than the Xtian commuinty on YT.

TheMajorDalsom compared Yokeup to a Nazi, writing:

> Yoke-up: Hitler Reflavored! Lawlz.

Although Crosisborg did not call Yokeup a 'racist' in this video nor describe his actions as violent, both comments developed categorizations of Yokeup as a 'Nazi'. Crosisborg's follow-up video entitled 'Yokeup Reaches New Low (Adult Language)' (V8) also developed explicit categorizations of Yokeup as a 'Nazi', further suggesting a relationship between being 'American white trash' and being a 'racist'. The comments about Yokeup, however, never pointed to any specific video or comment made by Yokeup to prove that he was, indeed, a racist.

Implicit negative categorization around Yokeup's socio-cultural identity was also present in responses to Yokeup, and PaulsEgo's video 'A Spotlight.' (V6) implied a negative evaluation based on Yokeup's socio-regional identity. In the video, after mocking Yokeup, PaulsEgo concluded by voicing sarcastic support for Yokeup and encouraging him to eat 'a nice spoonful of piping hot hate grits with butter'. By using a Southern US accent and referring to 'grits' (a food typical of working-class cuisine in the Southern United States), PaulsEgo associated Yokeup's socio-cultural identity with hatefulness. The implicit categorization of Yokeup therefore showed that category-bound activities or predicates were not always necessary for categorizations, and implicit category-bound predicates could be mobilized to categorize others. In these instances, the predicates were difficult to identify, but in user response, evidence from the inferences made could be seen in how users subsequently developed categories.

These descriptions of Yokeup were not simply, as Crosisborg claimed, 'bad', but represented categories of individuals who were likely to be viewed extremely negatively by most people in the YouTube audience and who were also associated with a negative Southern socio-cultural identity. Both were 'crazy', but in a particular sense of being bigoted and closed-minded individuals who were unable to engage in the YouTube community. The ability for PaulsEgo to make an implicit categorization of Yokeup based on his accent also revealed knowledge, resources, and prejudices that users held and which could be mobilized in drama interaction.

Shifts in use of metaphor and categorization of other users had direct impact on one another, with development of metaphor leading to new categorizations which, in turn, developed new metaphorical descriptions of Yokeup. The categorizations that resulted implied that Yokeup was the worst possible person, and a member of increasingly offensive categories. The implication of violence further described Yokeup as potentially dangerous. This contributed to the development of drama because Yokeup was subsequently not simply a Christian 'nutter' (as a commenter suggested) talking on YouTube, but a potentially violent individual. Users were then implicitly warned to avoid and disregard Yokeup, isolating him in the community and encouraging others to act negatively towards him.

The categorization devices of 'types of Christians'

Although there was an overwhelming negative response to Yokeup and his words, another argument emerged in response to Yokeup: was he or was he not a real Christian. This argument became one of the central disagreements of the drama, and reflected an incredibly diverse set of definitions of the category of 'Christian' – it was often used by different people to mean different things. Users distinguished between different 'types of Christians', creating their own category-bound activities and predicates to describe the different kinds of Christians. Although the category of 'Christian' was used in many different ways, it often appeared as a relational pair, with users differentiating between two kinds of 'Christians'. The category of 'Christian' was used in negative evaluations of others, and self-proclaimed 'believers' did not frequently refer to themselves or others as 'Christians', but rather categories derived from the Bible as well as Biblical metaphorical language.

The first use of the category of 'Christian' in relation to Yokeup occurred in the title to the video 'Yokeup: Poster Boy For Bad Christians' (V3), in which Crosisborg categorized Yokeup as a 'bad Christian' and then presented Yokeup's actions as category-bound activities of 'bad Christians'. Although Crosisborg's categorization of Yokeup as a 'bad Christian' appeared to imply that there were also 'good Christians', no users were explicitly categorized as 'good Christians' in Crosisborg's talk. Crosisborg not only presented Yokeup as a representative 'bad Christian', but also said that Yokeup's actions could be representative of Christian belief more generally. Crosisborg said,

> This is what shows me is so bad about Christianity … Yokeup is actually defending his position by saying, 'It's okay if I'm wrongly accusing these people of things. It's okay if I'm disregarding their faith and…I'm not looking past my own prejudices of my brand of Christianity. It's okay that I'm harassing and I'm causing them stress and I'm causing ill will and I'm defaming them because I'm forgiven in the end'. And yet he's the idiot.

In this description, Yokeup's actions were then presented as representative category-bound activities of 'Christians' rather than the 'bad Christians' mentioned in the video title, extending a description of Yokeup's actions as representative category-bound activities of all Christians.

By using the category 'bad Christian' rather than 'Christian' and describing Yokeup's actions as evidence of negativity in Christianity, Yokeup was not simply a 'Christian' like other Christians, but a 'bad Christian' who was behaving badly, a description that would likely appeal to a Christian audience. By omitting the category of 'good Christian', however, and suggesting that Yokeup showed what was 'so bad about Christianity', Crosisborg also presented the belief that Christianity was generally negative, appealing to his predominately non-Christian audience (as evidenced in the comments section). The use of 'bad Christian' and the omission of 'good Christian' allowed the audience to understand the video in two ways, both of which would result in supporting Crosisborg.

Crosisborg's use of the category of 'bad Christian' and the omission of a 'good Christian' category therefore showed the complexities of employing categories in a context that included both Christians and non-Christians. By categorizing Yokeup as a 'bad Christian' and referring in the course of the video to other Christians that Yokeup had 'harassed', the categorization potentially differentiated between Yokeup and other Christians on the site. At the same time, Crosisborg's claim that the action was representative of 'what's so bad with Christianity' described the actions as normative for the Christian category. Similar work by Fitzgerald and colleagues (Fitzgerald, 2012; Fitzgerald & Housley, 2007) shows how categories overlaid on individuals from their actions result in moral judgements and normative reasoning about the category in general. It also allowed for category inferencing (Sacks, 1995), suggesting that Yokeup's actions were the result of his Christian belief; that is, he acted wrongly *because* he was a Christian.

Crosisborg also purported to quote Yokeup's own justification for mistreating other Christians, but did so by exaggerating Yokeup's argument, speaking in the first person as Yokeup. Crosisborg highlighted how Yokeup was 'harassing' others and 'causing them stress', and only after a hyperbolic re-voicing did Crosisborg categorize Yokeup as an 'idiot'. Yokeup's treatment of others was next implicitly offered as a justification for Crosisborg's own categorizations of Yokeup, and Crosisborg's own offensive words were presented as having been provoked by Yokeup's insulting of others.

The re-voicing of the words of another user was another key element in the development of drama. Because Yokeup had posted his video and then removed it, viewers of Crosisborg's video may not have necessarily seen what Yokeup had originally said. The representation of what was said in the deleted videos, both by Crosisborg and subsequently by Yokeup, was an important way of influencing memories of past actions. With videos that were taken down from the site, the past actions of others were not fixed artefacts that users could reference, but malleable memories of the past that could be manipulated to serve particular purposes. In Crosisborg's video, the retelling of Yokeup's words presented Yokeup as more malicious. In Yokeup's retelling of his own words, he was only a faithful preacher of the Bible, sharing the good news.

This same pattern of presenting an exaggerated, hyperbolic pseudo-quotation of Yokeup before insulting him can be seen in the comments. th3d3wd3r wrote, 'It's the ultimate hypocrisy. "oh you're an atheist so you can sin without remorse". Then they can sin, repent and still get into heaven. Insane, really insane.' Like Crosisborg, th3d3wd3r re-voiced and exaggerated Yokeup's words before categorizing him, providing Yokeup's own words as justification for calling him 'insane'. PaulsEgo also employed descriptions of Yokeup's use of 'human garbage' to justify mocking him. Like Crosisborg and th3d3wd3r, PaulsEgo re-voiced Yokeup's words, saying, '[Yokeup] calls them human garbage ... Just comin' right out there and sayin' it there. Human garbage dumps; human garbage.' In all these cases, the words of Yokeup were not his actual words, but rather how another user perceived what he said, with the most offensive sense of the words highlighted.

Exaggerating Yokeup's words (and presenting his intentions as malicious before responding to him) was consistent in all negative responses to Yokeup. Any user could take what Yokeup had said and focus on what was the most offensive part and quote it to others without context as representative of Yokeup's discourse. This framing showed that within the community, speaking in an offensive way could be justified if users were able to present their response as provoked by another's more offensive words. The insults directed at Yokeup were supported and approved by others in the community who held Yokeup responsible for provoking the argument. As might be expected from Moor, Heuvelman, and Verleur's (2010) research showing that YouTube users saw 'flaming' on YouTube as often a response to perceived offence, users involved in the 'human garbage' drama worked to position their own 'flaming' as provoked by another user, and, therefore, as acceptable.

Crosisborg's categorization of Yokeup was then further extended in interaction by others, and devices produced in response to Crosisborg offered both new categories and category-bound activities. In both cases, the commenters reconfigured the device employed by Crosisborg, but followed the same pattern of presenting only negative evaluations of Christians. Two examples of these comments can be seen here. JACKtheRIPP3R189 wrote:

> "good christian" is a nonexistant thing. Someone can be good and christian, but if someone defines their being as "christian" then they are mentally unhealthy.

And LogicalSanity said:

> i think the title should be changed to "Yokeup: Poster Boy For Perfect Christians" That is exactly what a christian should be like. The vile things that come out of his mouth should be a red flag for the fake christians.

In both of the comments, users employed different categorization devices with complementary pairs of 'Christians' categories. JACKtheRIPP3R189 rejected the distinction between 'good' and 'bad Christian' as well as Crosisborg's categorization device. JACKtheRIPP3R189 removes the predicate 'good' from the category of 'Christian', suggesting instead that self-categorization of one's 'being' as 'Christian' was included in the predicate of being 'mentally unhealthy'. This distinction allowed for JACKtheRIPP3R189 to, like Crosisborg, make a moral judgement about Christianity more generally, while still conceding that Christians can be 'good'.

LogicalSanity's comment further reconfigured the categorization device in response to Crosisborg. In LogicalSanity's 'types of Christians' categorization device, two new categories were offered, 'perfect Christians' and 'fake Christians', with 'having vile things come out of their mouths' presented as a category-bound activity of 'perfect Christians'. LogicalSanity's use of 'fake Christian' also subverted Yokeup's frequent categorization of Christians he disagreed with elsewhere as 'fake' by evaluating the 'fake Christians' positively and the 'perfect Christians' negatively, like Crosisborg and JACKtheRIPP3R189. As with Crosisborg's categorization device, and LogicalSanity's categorization device in particular, the categories of 'perfect Christian' and 'fake Christians' had negative evaluations and implied a moral judgement. Although the implication was that 'fake Christians' are less offensive than 'perfect Christians' and that 'fake Christians' do not say vile things, the modifier 'fake' also implied negative category-bound activities and predicates. Within LogicalSanity's device, like the talk from Crosisborg, there were no 'good Christians', only Christians who say vile things and Christians who are fake.

The position of all three users was made clear in their categorization of Christians in negative ways, but also made concessions for the context of the drama, in which self-described Christians who also disagreed with Yokeup might be involved in the drama. The use of the categories (particularly using modifiers like 'bad', 'fake', and 'perfect') allowed for the users to negatively evaluate and condemn Yokeup (as well as other Christians behaving in a manner similar to him), but also allowed Christians to differentiate themselves from Yokeup by being different kinds of Christians. Although the discourse suggested a rejection of Christian belief, all the users allowed for the possibility that not all Christians were as offensive as Yokeup.

The use of the 'types of Christians' device also problematized the category of 'Christian' more generally, as what a 'Christian' is or should be was not uniformly agreed on in the discourse. Rather than serving as a description of a set of beliefs, 'Christian' served as part of the moral judgement of Yokeup. This negative evaluation of Christians was not accepted by all commenters. Although 'good Christian' was not explicit in Crosisborg's 'types of Christians' categorization device, 'good Christian' did appear in the categorization device of a Christian responding to Crosisborg. huskyfan1982, like the commenters above, also reconfigured the categories of 'good Christian' and 'bad Christian', while also challenging Crosisborg's ability as an atheist to categorize Christians. huskyfan1982, like the other commenters, also offered a reconfigured categorization device. huskyfan1982 wrote:

> First of all you are a swine and why Jezfreek and yokeup give any of you the time of day is beyond me (Matthew 7:6) Are they hitting on the most popular atheist for channel views? That would be wrong IMO. A spiritual man judges all things. Also do not judge based upon appearance but judge righteous judgment (John 7:24) Your reasoning ability on what a good Christian is, is laughable. God forbid when a atheists says, though you are a Christian, I like you. The world is to hate us-John 15:18.

In contrast to Crosisborg and the other comments, huskyfan1982 used a 'types of Christians' categorization device, which included 'bad Christian' as an implicit category and 'good Christian' as an explicit category. This 'types of

Christians' categorization device employed the same categories as Crosisborg, but the category-bound activities of 'good Christian' and 'bad Christian' were disputed and Biblical reference was used to describe a category-bound activity of 'good Christian': 'being hated by the world'. huskyfan1982's use of 'good Christian' was a clear response to Crosisborg's use of 'bad Christian' and the activities and predicates that Crosisborg employed. huskyfan1982's use of the scripture also shows an orientation towards the Biblical text as the authority for categorization rather than using the actions of other Christians, taking a stable text, and mobilizing in it a local context. Although the argument ostensibly remained about who was or was not a 'bad Christian', the differing uses of the categories and the different activities and predicates employed showed how the same categories could be used in the same context in disparate ways and to different effects.

The Biblical text was not only explicitly employed from the reference to Matthew 7.6, but also with the use of the Biblical register, referring to Crosisborg as a 'swine' (e.g. Proverbs 11.22, Matthew 8.30, Luke 15.16 in the King James Version), which implicitly appropriates authority to his categorization. Crosisborg's reasoning for categorization was rejected as 'laughable' and huskyfan1982 suggested that an atheist cannot make this categorization, further disputing Crosisborg's claim. Crosisborg was disqualified from categorizing 'Christians' as 'good' or 'bad' because his lack of belief in God limited his understanding of the Bible and made his implicit attempt to appeal to Christians irrelevant. If the Bible was the main authority for categorization, and Crosisborg did not employ the Bible in his categorization of Yokeup, then Crosisborg lacked the authority to categorize Yokeup as a 'bad Christian'.

The 'good Christian'/'bad Christian' distinction was made relevant by Crosisborg's video and the response of commenters to engage with the categorization, but the argument over 'good Christians' and 'bad Christians' and what authority the users appealed to differed. The argument around Crosisborg's categorization of Yokeup as a 'bad Christian' then suggests that even a stable category like 'Christian' could be used locally to different effects and with different meanings. In neither case did the user attempt to make a theological argument about belief in relation to the use of the categories, but instead employed category-bound activities and predicates that met the particular needs of the argument.

Like Yokeup, by categorizing users with Biblical language and reference, huskyfan1982 was able to re-voice the moral authority of the text. His categorization device, unlike Crosisborg's, was presented as being taken from the Bible (John 15.18), even though the passage was not directly quoted in the text. The passage quotes Jesus saying to his disciples, 'If the world hates you, keep in mind that it hated me first.' huskyfan1982's citation of the verse is then an extension of the Biblical text to the local situation, using words spoken to Jesus' disciples in the Bible to apply to all contemporary Christians on YouTube.

huskyfan1982's reference to John 15.18 and to the 'good Christians' category-bound activity of 'being hated by the world' also revealed an important insight about expectations regarding 'hate' in development of drama. Although 'being hated' might imply a negative evaluation, huskyfan1982's comment suggested the opposite: that being hated was actually positive because it was a category-bound activity of a 'good Christian'. huskyfan1982's comment showed that, for Christians, conflict with non-Christians that resulted in 'hate' may ultimately show one to be a 'good Christian', particularly if the 'hate' was the result of actions that were inspired by the Bible or God's word to an individual. Furthermore, huskyfan1982's metaphorical categorization of Crosisborg as a 'swine' showed the willingness of a Christian to provoke 'hate' using the Bible. In this way, calling Crosisborg a 'swine' was the same as Yokeup's presentation of human garbage as 'red ink', or the authoritative word of God. Neither was presented as a gratuitously insulting categorization because they employed the language and authority of the Bible.

Arguments about the category of 'Christian' and Yokeup's actions developed from Crosisborg's initial video in responses by others. Using a 'types of Christians' categorization device, philhellenes also presented Yokeup's actions as category-bound activities of a 'perfect Christian'. This process can be seen in the following extract from philhellenes' video, in which he said:

> You're the perfect Christian on YouTube no matter what the fluffy Christians say about the doctrine underpinning it all. They can't argue with you because you've got it on your side. The words are there; the book is there. The loving God that Anthony [jezuzfreek] talks about, the fluffy Jesus ... Certainly there are lines in there that are – in the Bible that are extremely fluffy. But underlining it all is the God that you worship.

philhellenes used a pair of categories, 'fluffy Christians' and 'perfect Christians', and the category-bound predicate of 'having the Bible on their side' for 'perfect Christians', to categorize Yokeup and negatively evaluate him. Yokeup was a 'perfect Christian' because he did what the Bible says, and his actions were then applied to the whole of the category of 'perfect Christians' making them category-bound activities. Like LogicalSanity's categorization device including 'perfect Christians' and 'fake Christians', philhellenes' 'types of Christians' categorization device included two 'Christian' categories, neither of which included a positive evaluation. The 'fluffy Christians', like 'fake Christians', were excluded from the hateful activities of the 'perfect Christians', but the metaphorical modifier 'fluffy' included a negative evaluation because Yokeup and others had described 'fluffy' Christians as those who were weak and avoided conflict with others. Also, because philhellenes said that 'perfect Christians' had the Bible 'on their side', the implication was that 'fluffy Christians' did not actually follow the Bible. This category-bound predicate furthered a negative evaluation not only of 'Christians', but also 'Christian' belief because it presented the Bible as the basis for Yokeup's offensive words. As in Crosisborg's categorization device, there were no 'good Christians' in philhellenes' talk.

Both support for and disagreement with philhellenes' categorization of Yokeup (and his implications about Christians more generally) were present in response to him in the comments section of his video. In particular, Christian commenters challenged philhellenes' categorization of Yokeup as a 'perfect Christian', seen in the following comment by the Christian user PenguinSymphony, who wrote:

> Whoa whoa this text is misinterpreted the tree and the branch and pruning is metaphoric for God burning sinners in hell (burning the branch) and encouraging those who spread the word of God (pruning the branch). I can c y u r angry at Yokeup but u shouldn't believe that christains despise those who r against their religion based on one man's misinterpretation. PenguinSymphony

In this comment, Yokeup's reading of John 15 was described as a misinterpretation of scripture and, therefore, not representative of 'Christians'. Based on this, the activity of 'despising those who are against their religion' was rejected as a category-bound activity for 'Christians'. PenguinSymphony did not categorize Yokeup explicitly, but rejected the argument made by philhellenes that being 'hateful' was a category-bound activity of 'Christian' because Yokeup had misinterpreted the text. The comment did not, however, explicitly reject Yokeup, only his interpretation of the Bible. In contrast to philhellenes and others using categorization to stereotype all Christians' actions, PenguinSymphony distinguished Yokeup from the category because he should be seen as an anomaly, someone just misreading the Bible.

Representation of the offensive words of some individuals as category-bound activities of the 'Christian' category was not limited to talk about Yokeup and, following the same pattern as Crosisborg and philhellenes, the negative actions of others were also used in the video entitled 'A Spotlight.' (V6). PaulsEgo used a 'types of Christians' categorization device that, like philhellenes' categorization device, also included the relational pair 'fluffy Christians' and 'Christians'. However, while philhellenes and Crosisborg modified the category of 'Christian', PaulsEgo categorized Yokeup and the Westboro Baptist Church simply as 'Christians' who behave in hateful ways and use the Bible to support their words and/or actions. These 'Christians' were then contrasted with 'fluffy Christians' who 'hide the truth of Christianity'. PaulsEgo said:

> He calls them 'human garbage' … and before you go and make an angry comment on his video not to dissuade you from doing that because he certainly deserves them. But uh just know that he backs that up with scripture all the way. And I'll let you go watch his video … Just let it be known that those words are right there in the Bible. Uh 'human garbage'.

PaulsEgo suggested that Yokeup illustrated Christian willingness to behave in ways that PaulsEgo felt were offensive. PaulsEgo mocked Yokeup's attempt to allocate the offence his words caused to the Bible by focusing on the use of 'human garbage dumps' and then saying, 'Just know that he backs that up with scripture'. PaulsEgo's comments, saying that Yokeup deserved 'angry comment(s)' showed PaulsEgo's rejection of the Bible's authority as well as the use of the term. PaulsEgo also stated that the words 'human garbage' were in the Bible, showing that Yokeup's development of metaphor vehicles were perceived as indistinguishable from the Bible. PaulsEgo then used the development to provide further evidence that Yokeup was willing to say or do anything provided he believed that the Bible supported him.

PaulsEgo described the actions of both the Westboro Baptist Church and Yokeup as 'spewing out unadulterated hatred' before saying,

> They are shining a fuckin spotlight on everything that is dirty and depraved and disgusting and wrong about Christianity and they're doing it from the inside . . . these are Christians from the inside out.

Yokeup and the Westboro Baptist Church are then equated with one another, 'Christians from the inside out', and their offensive words are category-bound activities of 'Christian'. PaulsEgo's contrast between 'Christians' and 'fluffy Christians' presented Yokeup and the Westboro Baptist Church as representative of the 'Christian' category. By not modifying 'Christian' in the pair of 'fluffy Christians' and 'Christians', PaulsEgo also did not allow for any positive evaluation of 'Christian'. 'Fluffy Christians' were weak people who liked the warm aspects of Christianity, and hid the truth of Christianity, while 'Christians' behaved in hateful ways.

While both philhellenes and Crosisborg had interaction with the Christian user jezuzfreek777 and appeared to make concessions that not all Christians should be negatively evaluated, PaulsEgo took a harder line without explicitly attempting to maintain a connection to jezuzfreek777 or any other Christian users. Each user therefore interacted with others in the community in different ways. Whether atheists or Christians or users who did not employ either label, what users wanted from others in terms of social interaction influenced the positions they took at any given time. For the atheist users who wanted to maintain positive relationships with some Christians in the community, simply denouncing all Christians was not an option.

As with philhellenes' video, commenters on 'A Spotlight.' (V6) used 'types of Christians' categorization devices similar to PaulsEgo's, and relexicalized the categories. For example, Yokeup and the Westboro Baptist Church were categorized as 'real Christians' and 'authentic Jesus worshipers'. The user TovChapaev contrasted 'people like Yokeup' and 'fundies' with 'wishy washing revisionist Christian types', establishing a category-bound activity for 'wishy-washy Christians' as 'having not read the Bible'. Although the specific names of the categories were changed, similar categories and category-bound activities had only negative evaluations of Christians and presented Yokeup and the Westboro Baptist Church as representative of a 'Christian' category.

Resistance to negative evaluation of all Christians was also present in responses to PaulsEgo's video, and his device was rejected by commenters who constructed new 'types of Christians' devices. Largo64 and cdavis9999 both suggested that 'Christians' would reject 'Yokeup and Fred Phelps' (the leader of the Westboro Baptist Church) as not 'Christian'. In this 'types of Christians' device, a new pair of 'Christians' is offered: 'false Christians' and 'Christians'. The user Vezoksfriend also wrote, 'I don't even want to call them christians', instead categorizing Yokeup and the Westboro Baptist Church as 'fundamentalist assholes', a negative categorization that drew a distinction between 'fundamentalists' and 'Christians'. Commenters also challenged the 'Christian' category-bound activity of 'acting in a hateful way' by suggesting that atheists act in a similar way. crazylaughscomedy challenged PaulsEgo more directly, saying, 'Whats the diference between you saying christians are 100% evil and youkup saying atheists are scum?" PaulsEgo's categorization device and the category-bound activity of 'hateful action' were then rejected because non-Christians also behaved in the same way. If atheists also act hatefully, then the action could not be used in a categorization device differentiating between the two.

Describing the actions of individual users as representative category-bound activities of particular categories was, as I have shown, frequent in the dataset. 'Types of Christians' categorization devices were made possible through presenting Yokeup as a representative of the category of 'Christian' and using his actions as category-bound activities of 'Christians', particularly given Yokeup's insistence that he was only repeating the words of the Bible. For non-Christians, Yokeup's offensive words and actions were used to negatively evaluate and present all Christians as either hateful, or 'fake Christians' and 'false Christians', hiding the 'real' Christianity. Atheists like philhellenes and PaulsEgo were able to then present a negative evaluation of 'Christianity' rather than simply rejecting the actions of a single user. Christian commenters disputed these 'types of Christians' categorization devices, arguing that Yokeup was not a representative Christian and that using his actions as category-bound activities of 'Christian' was, therefore, not acceptable. Both responses led to moral judgement, and drama surrounding the categories consequently continued because users disagreed and challenged the opinions and reasoning of others.

Although Yokeup's description of Crosisborg as 'garbage' was an attempt to limit Crosisborg's ability to befriend other Christians, as I showed in the analysis of metaphor, calling others 'human garbage' was viewed negatively, and users made connections between Yokeup and the actions and words of violent people, including Hitler. The comparison suggested that Yokeup's offensive words would lead to violence and he should be stopped. Attempting to silence Yokeup by directly challenging him was, therefore, common in responses to Yokeup. In the same way that Crosisborg's categorization of Yokeup as 'insane' attempted to delegitimize Yokeup's voice, philhellenes' categorization of Yokeup as a 'psychopath' attempted to impede Yokeup's message. philhellenes' response not only described Yokeup's opinion as wrong, but as the result of a 'lack of empathy' for others that Yokeup felt was supported by God and the Bible. By calling Yokeup a 'psychopath' and telling the story of the *Titanic*, philhellenes suggested that Yokeup needed to be stopped.

As in Crosisborg's video, commenters on the 'YouTube's Psychopath: Yokeup.' (V5) video page also engaged and developed philhellenes' descriptions of Yokeup as a 'psychopath', and redeployed Yokeup's description of others as 'human garbage' to Yokeup himself. Commenters repeated philhellenes' description of Yokeup also calling him 'filth' and 'shit', and developed vehicles to categorize Yokeup, including 'rubbish', 'scumbag', 'scum', and 'douche(bag)'. By subverting 'garbage' and applying it back to Yokeup, the action of the categorization was then also applied to Yokeup, delegitimizing him in the same way that philhellenes talked about Yokeup as delegitimizing others. The repetition of offensive language served to support philhellenes' claim that Yokeup should be silenced.

Within Christian interaction, the Bible was consistently invoked when users disagreed about the categorizations of others, but categories of denominational affiliation (such as Catholic and Lutheran) were infrequent. Only nine unique institutional categories were identified in the whole video page corpus: Catholic, Calvinist, Baptist, Quaker, Unitarian, Westboro Baptist, Protestant, Mormon, and Puritan. On further investigation, a majority of denominational categories appeared in lists of different belief systems when commenters were arguing that all belief systems were the essentially the same. Categorization using a denominational affiliation, either of self or others, was completely absent, and denominational disagreements were never invoked.

A key exception was the category of 'fundamentalist', which occurs twelve times in the video page corpus. Although historically a Christian movement (Nagata, 2001), in the dataset 'fundamentalist' was used with negative category-bound activities rather than category-bound predicates of belief or church membership. Furthermore, 'fundamentalist' was not used by Christians in discourse about others and no one in the video page corpus self-identified as a 'fundamentalist'. This corroborates with other research that found Evangelical Christians avoid the term in self-categorization (Malley, 2004; Nagata, 2001) and it also appears linked to the Evangelical avoidance of denominational labels in self-categorization, a finding that corroborates Malley's findings from ethnographic interviews of Evangelical Christians (Malley, 2004). Instead, the use of 'fundamentalist' reflected the occasioned nature of categorization within the community because 'fundamentalist' was not limited to discussing the negative actions of Christians in the community. PurushaDesa wrote:

> Well antitheism deals with the immorality with theism. Atheism alone deals with logic and rationality. There's absolutely no truth in this 'atheist fundamentalist' label of causation at this moment in time. Aggressively arguing a point about immoral theisms is certainly not akin to actual Christian, Muslim and Jewish fundamentalism. It's a theoretical possibility, but the people given this label like Dawkins, Hitchens and Harris don't preach violence and hatred as they do.

PurushaDesa differentiated between categories by saying that a 'fundamentalist' 'preaches violence and hatred', whereas an 'atheist' 'deals with logic and rationality' and argues points 'about immoral theisms'. In this context, the categorization included a category-bound activity of 'preaching violence and hatred', rather than category-bound predicates of belief or institutional affiliation. The use of 'fundamentalist' to describe hateful actions rather than belief highlighted a consistent trend in three drama exchanges for categorization devices to differentiate between users based on differing category-bound activities rather than category-bound predicates such as belief or ethnic or socio-political identity. With the exception of 'American white trash', focus was almost exclusively on the actions of the categorized user.

The lack of institutional categories as well as the adaptation of the category of 'fundamentalist' shows two important aspects of interaction in the 'human garbage' drama. First, Christians foregrounded categories and categorization devices from the Bible rather than their own denominational affiliations, highlighting the Bible's importance in Christian interaction in the dataset. Second, adaptation of 'fundamentalist' showed that some categories could have very different contextual meanings, depending on who was using the category and for what purpose. 'Fundamentalist', a category that has historically been a denomination of 'Christian', could potentially be used to categorize anyone using a comparison of shared category-bound activities.

The avoidance of denominational categories in favour of Biblically derived categories contributed to the development of drama because it allowed users to argue about what was or was not appropriate for those who claimed to be 'Christian' or 'believers'. Yokeup's categorization of others, and particularly his eventual claim that everyone was either a 'believer' or 'garbage', contributed to the development of drama because users who were self-proclaimed Christians were categorized as 'enemies of God' based on their actions. Yokeup's use of the Biblical categories 'friends of the world' and 'enemies of God' further dictated what was acceptable for Christians in terms of friendship with non-Christians through his description of category-bound activities of 'believers'. The challenging of others' often implicit self-categorization led to angry responses to Yokeup furthering the development of drama. As users opposed Yokeup, his response was to read again from the Bible and assert the moral authority of the text in his categorizations.

The discussions about who was and was not a Christian also occurred in talk by Christians, but the language of the discussion was often quite different. Rather than focus on the word 'Christian', the Christians in the dataset (and particularly Yokeup) used Biblical and religious language to talk about distinction between different kinds of Christians, as seen in his differentiation between 'religious' users and 'saved' users. Yokeup said, in his video 'I doubt JezuzFreek is saved . . .',

> But one interesting thing that I've been thinking about . . . I wonder if jezuzfreek is saved. I wonder if he's had a salvation moment. I wonder if Paula's saved, if she's had a salvation moment. And you know, I-I wonder about a lot of people, a lot of people that claim to be Christians. And it seems to be a theme in the Baptist community . . . Are they religious, or are they saved? Have they-have they had that moment when the Holy Spirit comes

into their heart? In *hislivingsacrifice*'s Paula's video, you know she talked about church . . . and she said, 'You know, it's more like a fashion show.' And-and it's kind of struck me: are you going to church to be seen, are you going to church to hear the word of God? You know, we preach down at the truck stop every Sunday. Ain't no fashion show. It's people hungry to hear the word of God.

Here, Yokeup spoke about two other users in the community, jezuzfreek777 and hislivingsacrifice. In describing the users, Yokeup employed two categories – 'religious' and 'saved '– and used the category-bound activity of 'having a salvation moment' to differentiate between the two. Yokeup did not explicitly place himself or either of the other users in the categories, but, much like the talk we have seen so far, appeared to be differentiating between two kinds of Christians, without the 'Christian' category to differentiate between them. Instead, Yokeup employed categories from within the Evangelical Christian community to describe the differences among users.

The categories 'saved' and 'religious' serve as a kind of relational pair, much in the way we have seen categories like 'good Christians' and 'bad Christians'. Yokeup attempts to make a differentiation between two kinds of people that might otherwise be seen as occupying the same category by asking, 'Have they had that moment when the Holy Spirit comes into their heart?' To be saved then is to 'have a salvation moment' when the 'Holy Spirit comes into your heart', focusing on the conversion experience of an individual, rather than their own assertion that they are Christians. The 'religious' category is then established through suggesting that Paula and jezuzfreek777 are religious, but not saved, first through the statement 'I wonder if jezuzfreek is saved', which uses thought representation to suggest that jezuzfreek777 and Paula might not be saved, and by grouping Paula, Paula's church, a lot of people that claim to be Christians, and the Baptist community together. Yokeup represented Paula's voice as saying that her church is more like a 'fashion show', building a distinction that the viewer could infer between going to church to be seen (the religious) and going to church to 'hear the word of God' (the saved).

This distinction between going to church 'to be seen' and going to church 'to hear the word of God' is, of course, not observable, but rather allows Yokeup to make a judgement about others based on his perception of their intentions. He added another category-bound activity, saying members of the saved category not only attend church to 'hear the word of God', but they were also 'hungry for it', a metaphorical description of intention that was again not observable, but drew a contrast between himself and the others, using the categories he had established. Religious people show false piety and are vain, whereas the truly pious were inwardly eager for spiritual truth and did not care about how they looked. The evidence for both was in their outward appearance. Although Yokeup did not claim to be saved, the viewer could infer it by how he presents himself and the truckstop church as inversely related to the other 'religious' users.

Inference was key to this segment as Yokeup did not say any person is explicitly 'saved' or 'religious', only created the apparatus for making the categorization, leaving the viewer to do the categorization themselves. By setting up the categories and allowing the viewer to infer the conclusion, Yokeup distanced himself from the categorizations. Yokeup, throughout his videos, encouraged viewers to 'check it out' for themselves in the Bible; that is, to see if what he had said correlates with the Bible. By doing this, Yokeup appealed to the Bible's authority, potentially adding more strength to his argument, but also distancing himself from his claims, as he presented himself as only saying what is written in the Bible.

The video comments showed that although the categories of saved and religious were accepted among some commenters, Yokeup's category-bound activities and membership rules are potentially different. One commenter wrote,

> Jeff [Yokeup], saved people can become religious and religious people can get saved. I don't doubt Jesusfreek is truly saved, I may not agree with him on everything he says but I have listened to him enough to know he has a relationship with God and have heard him talk about his born again experience.

In this case, the commenter seemed to be applying a different description to being 'born again': having a relationship with God. This, the commenter argued, could be evidence of jezuzfreek777 being truly saved. It was also important to recognize that the categories that Yokeup employed were the result of online, real-time text production. Although he relied on standardized categories employed by fundamentalist Christians (evidenced in the acceptance of the categories in the comments), how the categorization emerged did not appear to be planned, but was dynamic, dependent on real-time talk, and potentially negotiated in the comments section and subsequent videos or in responses by users both aligned with and opposed to the user.

As we have seen above, many of the category-bound activities, and indeed the categories themselves, were metaphors or contain metaphorical language. The metaphors of 'hungry', 'saved', and the Holy Spirit 'coming into your heart' are used to describe the category that is itself a metaphor: 'saved'. Inversely, Yokeup used the 'fashion show' metaphor to describe the negative church-going practices of the 'religious'. Metaphor use, much like Yokeup's indirect categorization statements, created the affordance of ambiguity, allowing Yokeup to speak in imprecise terms about categories and having the effect of categorizing others. For instance, whether or not those that attended the truckstop church congregation were indeed more 'hungry' for the 'word of God' than those in Paula's church was impossible to say, but the description of one category as 'hungry' for 'God's word' and the other as taking part in a 'fashion show' allowed the viewer to infer that those attending the truckstop church were doing the right thing and those attending Paula's church were not.

The 'saved' and 'salvation' metaphors also brought with them an implicit pairing of 'saved' with 'saviour' in the event of 'being saved', a set of conventional metaphors and categories. By using the metaphors of being 'saved' and 'salvation', Yokeup mobilized a system of relationships and events, of which community members would be aware (Eglin & Hester, 2003). The 'saved' metaphor also provided the affordance of narrowing and broadening inclusion rules. Although both Paula and jezuzfreek777 may have described themselves as 'saved', Yokeup's use of the category and his interpretation of their actions allowed him to question their category membership. Unlike formal membership rules in formal religious institutions, using the 'saved' metaphor to describe someone could be interpreted and defined differently depending on the speaker's position. The data suggests that the category of 'saved' was applied differently by different speakers.

Metaphor use later in the video also created ambiguity around the actions that might make someone 'religious' rather than 'saved'. Yokeup mentioned that jezuzfreek 'hangs out' with the wrong friends, suggesting that jezuzfreek was 'friends' with the wrong people, but not clarifying what was wrong or unacceptable about 'hanging out' with atheists and non-Christians, as 'sharing the gospel' with non-Christians was an important part of Yokeup's Evangelical worldview. The metaphorical action of 'hanging out' suggested that jezuzfreek had done something wrong without specifying exactly what was not acceptable about the action.

The metaphor use created debate about the category-bound activities of the 'saved', as one commenter mentioned that Jesus 'hung out' with sinners. In this case, because Jesus' actions were seen as prototypical good behaviour of the 'saved', 'hanging out' with 'sinners' (or non-Christians more generally) should not be rejected as an unacceptable action. Yokeup, in the comments section of 'I doubt JezuzFreek is saved...', argued:

> Amen, and what did Jesus do when He hung out with them?? care to share those details...did Jesus condone their sins, continue to hang out with them for years while they lived in sin? well, did HE?

For Yokeup, the purpose of 'hanging out' with non-Christians and 'sinners' was not to 'condone their sin', suggesting that jezuzfreek has done so, while Yokeup himself has not. Instead, Yokeup's actions were entirely acceptable, while the actions of others were not.

The ambiguity of the metaphor and its usefulness as a means to differentiate between users broke down when users attempted to understand the meaning of the metaphor. The commenter MrTh1rteen, in an effort to clarify the metaphor, wrote, 'He did continue to "hang out" (Don't think that's an accurate phrase, sry 4 using it) while they were in sin because they were Always in sin He never once condoned any of their sins. The fact is Jesus preached to ALL, he didn't keep himself away from people who were demonic.' Again, metaphor use seems to create ambiguity around category-bound activities, allowing users to both agree that Jesus did not 'hang out with sinners', but disagree on the meaning of 'hang out'.

Metaphor use both in terms of categories and category-bound activities became a way for users to avoid resolving the drama, as users could argue back and forth about the meanings of the words and what was or was not acceptable. Users could attack others while still maintaining some plausible deniability in what they were actually claiming about others. Furthermore, the issue of authority and the meaning of the categories was particularly important in the use of categories from the Bible, which I will now investigate.

The role of the Bible in categorization and interaction

Disagreements over the use and meaning of categories then extended to Biblical categories, which were also often interpreted in different ways, with users employing the same language to describe different people and actions. Like disagreement about Biblical metaphorical language, categories derived from the Bible exposed disagreements among Christians about Biblical interpretation and often exasperated underlying disagreements among users. However, although users (particularly Christians) disputed the categorizations and argued about the meaning of particular Biblical texts, they did so without disputing the moral authority of the Bible.

As I mentioned above, arguments about John 15 and categorization devices derived from the passage centred on how the parable could be used to produce devices for both believers and non-believers. In the video entitled 'John 15 for Dummies – Unbelievers are human garbage?' (V12), christoferL read directly from the Bible and distinguished between people using two metaphorical categories contained in the John 15 parable: 'branches that bear fruit' and 'withered branches.' By reading from the Bible, christoferL's categorization device was also derived from the same parable that Yokeup presented to categorize others as 'human garbage'. In contrast to Yokeup, who had used language from the parable to categorize Crosisborg, christoferL argued that, because Jesus was speaking only to his disciples in John 15, the categories from the parable could not be applied to 'unbelievers'. christoferL explicated the passage, saying:

> Jesus is the vine and his followers are the branches. If we remain in him, we will bear much fruit, but without him we can do nothing. We are fruitless. If we do not remain in him, we are thrown away and wither only to be burnt up. Now, really the key here is remaining in him. An unbeliever is never in him. Only a believer can be considered in him and only a believer can remain in him as unbeliever cannot remain where he has never been.

christoferL emphasized the category-bound activity of 'not remaining in him' for 'withered branches' and stated that this category-bound activity could not apply to 'unbelievers' because 'unbelievers' were never considered 'in [Christ]'. christoferL, therefore, argued that John 15 could only be used in categorizations of 'believers', not 'unbelievers'. By rejecting the possibility that an 'unbeliever' could be categorized as a 'withered branch', christoferL implicitly rejected Yokeup's categorization of 'unbelievers' as 'human garbage'. The basis for this challenge was, however, Yokeup's exegesis of scripture rather than his use of the category 'human garbage', which christoferL did not comment on in the video. christoferL argued instead that Yokeup had used the parable in the wrong way by ignoring the context of the passage.

How users interpreted the metaphorical categories from the parable in the YouTube context was central to the disagreement among users in the community. Throughout his video, christoferL applied the language of the parable to categorization in the YouTube context. In the relexicalization of 'believer' from 'follower of Christ' and 'disciple', the Biblical categories derived from the text were applied to users in the community through the metaphorical category-bound activity of 'remaining in [Christ]'. Through use of the Biblical categories, christoferL presented his rejection of Yokeup as derived from the Bible. Particularly through reading from John 15 before giving his interpretation, christoferL presented his own words as an extension of the Biblical text, in the same way that Yokeup also read from the Bible before presenting his relexicalization of 'withered branches' as 'human garbage'.

Within the same video, christoferL presented a second device to distinguish between all people. christoferL emphasized that 'being burned' was a category-bound activity of 'unbelievers' by stating: 'This isn't to say that unbelievers won't burn because unfortunately you guys you will if you don't accept Christ'. In this statement, a 'believers/unbelievers' categorization device reinforced the Biblically-derived category-bound activities of 'believers' and 'unbelievers': 'believers' 'accept Christ and go to heaven', while 'unbelievers' 'do not accept Christ and burn in hell'. christoferL asserted that even if John 15 did not, by itself, make this point, the activity of 'burning' still applied to unbelievers.

christoferL's emphasis that 'unbelievers' will burn also appeared to serve as an attempt to clarify his belief in a literal interpretation of hell for a Christian audience. In the comments, another Christian user, Elizabeth01010101, who had not viewed the entire video, voiced concern that christoferL might not have been explicit enough in telling unbelievers that they will burn if they do not accept Christ, writing, 'I do think you should have added that unbelievers go to hell. This video could be interpreted as if unbelievers have no consequence', to which christoferL responded, 'At 4:10 [4:10 is a reference to the time code in the video] – I said "This isn't to say unbelievers won't burn – because unfortunately you guys – you will if you don't accept Christ" – I thought that would suffice . . . maybe I should add an annotation?' By showing an eagerness to stress the point that unbelievers 'burn', christoferL maintained a position that hell should be understood literally; a position recognized and supported by other Christians. Like Crosisborg's categorization of 'bad Christians', christoferL showed an interest in appealing to both Christian and non-Christian audiences who could view his actions as both more caring than Yokeup's, but still as maintaining the meaning of the Bible.

Support for christoferL (including his use of 'believer/unbelievers' and the emphasis on 'being burned') as well as for his implicit rejection of Yokeup's 'human garbage' category can be seen in the acceptance by the commenters. Users praised the video, saying, for example, that christoferL had spoken 'simply and truthfully' as well as calling the video a 'Great message', 'right on', a 'great job', and a 'good video'. Although the majority of comments were positive, some resistance to the category-bound activity of 'burning' can be observed when the Christian user RJL738 praised christoferL as a 'compassionate person' and another Christian, huckster271, responded, writing: '@RJL738 as compationate as anyone who condones the "burning" of anyone can be'. The presence of both positive and negative comments highlighted the fact that there was no single accepted approach to Biblical exegesis and use of the scripture was consistently debated.

Disputes over readings of the Bible were ongoing in the 'human garbage' drama. In response to christoferL, Yokeup's video entitled 'more on . . . human garbage' (V14) categorized even more users by reference to the parable of the vine and branches, and also employed an 'unbelievers/believers' categorization device including the same pair of categories as christoferL. Unlike christoferL, however, Yokeup argued that the categorization device derived from the John 15 parable could be applied to everyone, not just Christians. In Yokeup's talk, because the categories of 'unbelievers' and 'believers who do not remain in Christ' share the category-bound activity of being 'burned', they were equivalent, both being 'withered branches'. Disagreement about devices stemmed in part from the ambiguous use of Biblical language. The precise meaning of the category-bound activity of 'remaining in Christ' or 'remaining connected to Christ' was never resolved, despite a suggestion later in the chapter that 'remaining in Christ' referred to 'obeying [Christ's] commands' (John 15.10). Although the activity was drawn from the Bible, the lack of a clear, concrete action associated with the metaphor (apart from 'obeying Jesus' commands') allowed Yokeup to describe others' actions as evidence they were 'not connected to Christ' or 'not bearing good fruit'. For users who shared the same exegesis of the Bible, the meaning was clear and did not require any further description. For Christians with different understandings of the same passage or who did not share the same exegesis, Yokeup had misread the passage, and his subsequent words were unacceptable.

Challenges also led Christians to engage in further exegesis of the Bible to support their claims. In his response to christoferL, in 'more on...human garbage', Yokeup not only reiterated his reading of John 15, but continued to relexicalize 'human garbage' with new categories. In developing categorizations, Yokeup continued to employ the privileged voice of the Bible as the 'word of God', adding legitimacy to his own words. The voice of the Bible was both explicit, in the direct quotation, and implicit as in the development of metaphorical language from the Bible. For example, Yokeup read from James 4 to support his categorization of other users as 'garbage':

> If you think the believers are considered garbage, if they disconnect ... James chapter four verse four, 'Adulterers and adulteresses. Do you not know that friendship with the world is enmity with God? Whoever therefore wants to be a friend of the world, makes himself an enemy of God.'

Yokeup used James 4:4 to further support his categorization of others as 'garbage'. Yokeup first presented additional Biblical categories: 'friends of the world' and 'enemies of God' from James 4. Then, using the shared category-bound activities of the categories 'friend of the world' and 'enemy of God' from James 4, Yokeup categorized all 'ooshy-gooshy' Christians who want to be 'friends of the world' as 'enemies of God'. In addition to presenting a negative evaluation of many Christians, Yokeup's categorization of some users as 'ooshy-gooshy, wishy-washies', 'friends of the world', and 'enemies of God' again were treated the same as the categories of 'Christians who do not remain in Christ' and 'unbelievers' as 'garbage'. Yokeup applied the category-bound activity of 'being burned' and 'garbage' to both 'believers who do not remain in Christ' and 'unbelievers', using a categorization device in which all users and people were either 'people who are connected to Christ' or 'people who are not connected to Christ'.

As with christoferL's video, general praise for Yokeup can be seen in the comments section, including, 'Amen brother, Amen......' and 'Preach it Brother.' Commenters also repeated and developed the 'believer' category, relexicalizing it as 'the elect, the saved, the true church' and 'saved people' or employing it as part of a relational pair with 'false Christians'. The repetition and development of categories similar to other conventionalized categories showed that Yokeup's distinction between two kinds of 'believers' was understood and accepted among some of the viewers.

Although comments were generally supportive of Yokeup, resistance was also present in the comments section. The Christian user dreamwarrior2008 challenged Yokeup, particularly the category-bound activity of 'enemies of God' as 'wanting to be friends with the world' seen here:

> so are you saying that when jesus was being friends with tax collectors, prostitutes and others that that was wrong?

Yokeup responded to this with:

> what did Jesus say to them about their sin when He hung out with them? remember that part? and by the way, Jesus did nothing wrong

dreamwarrior2008 used the categories 'tax collectors' and 'prostitutes' as examples of 'unbelievers' with whom Jesus was friends, the comment challenged Yokeup's relexicalization of 'friend of the world' as 'enemy of God', using the activity of Christ as prototypical good activity. In response, Yokeup (under the username 'YokedtoJesus') agreed with the presentation of Jesus' actions as prototypical, writing that Jesus 'did nothing wrong', but maintained the imprecise categories and category-bound activities explicated in the video by saying that 'friendship' with 'unbelievers' is not acceptable as although Jesus 'hung out' with sinners, he was not their 'friend'. By continuing to describe the category-bound activities of 'friend of the world' in metaphorical language, Yokeup rejected dreamwarrior2008's challenge without rejecting the actions of Jesus.

Yokeup, in the course of the drama, continued to use the Bible to categorize other Christians, drawing on Bible passages for authority in describing the actions of others. In his video 'Straight up ... Wolves and Garbage. call it what it is' (V16), Yokeup used a passage from Ezekiel 22 to describe some Christians as 'wolves':

> I mean at some point in time you have to say, 'Hey there's a wolf. There's a wolf.' And the wolf's mission is to seek and destroy and to pull people away. And a lot of it has to do with justifyin' their own sin. A lot of it has to do with sayin', 'Hey you're— your sin life is okay. It's okay to be a gay Christian. It's okay to be an adulterous Christian. It's okay to get drunk...' It...doesn't preach obedience and submission and surrender and being a slave to Jesus Christ. It goes the other direction of allowance and sayin', 'Oh, it's okay to vote for Obama you know. Look, it's okay, and oh abortion in some cases, well it's okay.' It opens up that door. Those are wolves. Those are absolute wolves.

This video from Yokeup brought together many of the key issues in the drama in one extract, employing metaphorical categories, categories derived from the Bible, and category-bound activities. 'Wolf' in the original passage is part of a prophecy and does not explicitly relate to an individual or group of people, but rather to people who 'destroy souls'. Yokeup then takes the passage and, as he did with the John 15 parable, relates the text to the 'human garbage' drama by using 'wolf' to describe others in the community. For Yokeup, the text of the Bible can and should be applied to the drama situation and provides a useful frame to users to understand his actions and the actions of others.

The 'wolf' that Yokeup describes in the passage has the mission to 'seek and destroy and to pull people away', which appears to be an allusion to both the passage ('to shed blood and destroy souls') and John 10:10, in which Jesus refers to a thief who 'comes only to steal and kill and destroy'. The imprecision of the allusion and the original source of the 'wolf' prophecy (Ezekiel 22) allowed Yokeup to apply the category to others in the community. While the activity of the 'wolf' in the text was 'to destroy souls', Yokeup extends the action to the metaphorical activity 'pull people away' and applies this to any action he considers to be 'sinful', including being gay, voting for Obama, or supporting abortion.

These activities that Yokeup lists are, in and of themselves, unrelated, but instead make sense in terms of the larger overall drama occurring among the users. Support for Obama and abortion rights are both positions that Pastor Javid, another Christian in the community, took. By listing these activities as 'pulling people away from God', Yokeup implicitly categorizes Javid as a 'wolf'.

Without explicitly saying that Javid is a wolf, other users in the community who understand the context of the disagreement (and indeed, Javid himself) would be able to understand the implicit claim that Yokeup is making.

The 'calling out' of 'wolves' in the community also implicitly categorizes Yokeup as a 'watchman', a role that he explicitly talked about taking at other times, by referring to the Biblical passage of Ezekiel 33, in which the prophet is appointed as a 'watchman' over 'God's people'. Yokeup, by saying, 'There's a wolf', describes himself not as someone attacking others, but someone who protects the community from dangerous individuals. He is not taking issue with the actions of others for entertainment or to get revenge, but rather because, as he describes, he is a 'watchman' caring for others.

In this talk, Yokeup was careful to not explicitly call anyone a 'wolf' by name, a pattern that he also followed in the discussion of who was an 'enemy of God'. Yokeup's categorization of other self-described Christians as 'friends of the world' and 'enemies of God' was carefully hedged and allocated offence to the Bible, making it appear that Yokeup was not attacking anyone, but rather, as with the Ezekiel 22 passage, simply repeating what the Bible said. Yokeup avoided directly categorizing specific Christians, as seen here:

> When I hear people like Christopher or Javid or any of those wishy-washy ooshy-gooshies … Pastor Mike's in that crowd. Jerome Stein's definitely in that crowd...There's just a whole bunch of people that want to be friends or sell bar-b-que sauce or grow their subscription base or you know whatever. What's the objective? If you want to be a friend with the world, you will be an enemy of God.

Although the sequential structure of Yokeup's talk implied that the users he named were 'enemies of God' (particularly through the use of shared category-bound activities), the categorization was actually implicit. Yokeup never directly said that any individual user was an 'enemy of God', instead hedging his language by saying, 'People like Christopher or Javid'. Unlike Yokeup's initial insult of Crosisborg, Yokeup's treatment of Christians in this video avoided explicit categorization. Instead, Yokeup presented his words as directly following from the Bible, but required the hearer to construct the categorization. Just as christoferL took care in presenting the 'burning' of unbelievers, Yokeup's response and his careful use of the Bible suggested an attempt to maintain relationships with christoferL and other Christians even while acting in a way that could potentially be viewed negatively.

Changes in how Yokeup addressed others were evidenced in the comments section of 'more on...human garbage' (V14). Although Yokeup had attempted to avoid explicit categorization of christoferL in the video, commenters did not. The user mackiemoo addressed christoferL directly as well, saying, 'nice try Christofer the only one here that is a disgrace is you' as well as using the threat, 'I would like to kick him in the shins myself'. Yokeup also used offensive metaphorical descriptions of christoferL directly in the comments, writing, 'Christofer doesn't have back-bone, no spine for the fight for Jesus and what is right'. Yokeup and others were, in this instance, more aggressive towards christoferL, and although the comments were also public, Yokeup appeared to be more willing to aggressively challenge christoferL in the comments section than the video.

In commenter response to Yokeup's videos, no one suggested that Yokeup's use of 'garbage' should be viewed negatively and commenters also agreed and reinforced Yokeup's presentation of potentially offensive Biblical language as 'God's word', which was authoritative. Users commented, 'Yeah, everyone should check out the word of God for themselves', and 'I think gods word is clear on this matter', showing support for Yokeup's categorizations of others. The lack of strongly offended responses to his video, however, must take into account Yokeup's censorship since he explicitly moderated the comments, possibly deleting those that disagreed with him. Still, it was clear in these comments as well as from the rest of the video page corpus that at least some users did support and encourage Yokeup, holding similar beliefs and expectations about the Bible and what should or should not be viewed negatively.

The care taken to avoid presenting his words as an insult suggested that Yokeup was seeking positive face with other Christians in the community. Although he repeatedly claimed that the opinions of others were irrelevant, his response to some users in careful, hedged language showed that he was eager to be a positive influence among other Christians and to be regarded as an authority on scripture. At different times, Yokeup appeared to address others, both Christians and non-Christians, in different ways, sometimes treating them harshly and speaking aggressively towards them, and other times treating them in a friendly way. Changes in his interactions with and orientation towards others illustrated the dynamic nature of relationships in the community, in which users who opposed one another could eventually agree, and vice versa, changing their interactions with each other.

The extract also shows how the history of drama in the community played a role in how members viewed each other. Yokeup said, '. . . there's just a whole bunch of people that want to be friends or sell bar-b-que sauce', a reference to a time in the past when Javid had been selling bar-b-que sauce through his channel. The reference would be understood by members of the community with a shared knowledge of past interactions, and knowing what Yokeup was referring to, would allow users then the ability to interact further, either in the comments or in making a response video.

Throughout the drama, the systematic metaphor CHRISTIANS ARE MEMBERS OF THE SAME FAMILY was used by Christians. Nine of the eleven vehicles in the FAMILY grouping were either taken from direct quotes of Biblical text or used by Christians to refer to other Christians. FAMILY vehicles within this grouping appeared to be used primarily in describing God as a father and other users within the community as brothers or sisters in Christ. The FAMILY grouping shows how different kinds of systematicity can be present in metaphor use. The use of FAMILY metaphors can be described as a 'systematic metaphor', a 'scenario' like those described by Musolff (2006), or an extension of Biblical parables which describe the relationship between God and Christians in terms of familial relationships. Evidence supporting all three of these descriptions of systematicity in metaphor use could be applied to the use of FAMILY vehicles.

Use of the brother/sister in Christ could be observed particularly in Christian comments on other Christians' videos. FAMILY vehicles were primarily employed when users were praising the spiritual message of a video and encouraging the video maker, and showing emotional closeness and solidarity. An example of this pattern can be seen in a comment by joeXcel on christoferL's video titled 'We Can't Choose Our Brothers':

> Excellent message you shared ChristoferL. This is deep and will impact many on YT in/with their walk with Christ, and with each other. I have been reminded many, many times by brothers and sisters in Christ on YT that *we are 'Family'*.
>
> God bless you and Diana.

Here, joeXcel praised the message of christoferL's video and christoferL's positive impact on both Christian user spiritual experience as well as users' relationships with each other, metaphorized as a walk with Christ and other Christians. The relationship between Christian users was then metaphorized as fraternity and sorority, within the construct of the family. christoferL's use of FAMILY vehicles and the response by commenters suggested conventionalization given their ubiquity in the dataset.

As the title to christoferL's video 'We Can't Choose Our Brothers' (V2) suggested, FAMILY vehicles did not necessarily denote agreement or friendship, but shared belief and affiliation. Within the video, christoferL stated that arguments with other Christians did not make them any less brothers in Christ and christoferL literalized the FAMILY vehicles, discussing an argument with his own biological sister. Similarly, in the video titled 'more on. . .human garbage' (V14), Yokeup referred to christoferL as a little brother while criticizing christoferL's exegesis of scripture and his relationship with atheists on YouTube. In both these examples, FAMILY vehicles were applied to users that shared belief, but were not necessarily emotionally close.

The metaphorical vehicles comprising the FAMILY grouping alluded to the Biblical text, but not necessarily to a specific passage. As with the voice of God, descriptions of God as father are ubiquitous in the Bible, with different representations of this metaphor occurring throughout (e.g. Psalm 68.5, John 6.46, Romans 1.7). However, unlike the GOD SPEAKS TO CHRISTIANS systematic metaphor, atheist users responding to Yokeup, including Crosisborg, philhellenes, and PaulsEgo, did not engage the FAMILY metaphors in the same way as the voice of God metaphor. PaulsEgo's insulting of Yokeup in his video entitled 'A spotlight.' (V6) included a mocking reference to Yokeup as a 'brother' who has rejected him, a use that subverted the metaphor for humour. Cameron (2010b) has shown the value of metaphor appropriation in conciliation discourse bringing together former enemies by creating shared ownership of language; here, PaulsEgo's use shows that appropriation can be used to mock another and create distance.

Discussion

Metaphor use in categorization included both metaphorical categories and category-bound activities, and was often used to negatively evaluate others, particularly Yokeup. Like categorizations employing Biblical language, users interpreted metaphorical categories and category-bound activities in different ways and employed the same metaphorical categories in unique categorization devices. Use of metaphor in categorization of others, particularly those including a negative evaluation, contributed to the development of drama when subsequent discourse about a category developed the negative evaluations, often in escalating negative, offensive descriptions.

Lakoff (1987) has observed that in day-to-day interaction, categories do not cause difficulty for speakers because categories are thought to be 'common sense' constructions. The interaction in the 'human garbage' drama, however, shows how categorization can become complicated in contexts where speakers do not share a 'common sense'. The interaction of a diverse group of users within the community changed the immediate context in which categories were heard and understood and required users to interact with others who may regularly employ different categories or the same categories in different ways. Through categorization analysis, investigating the constituent parts of category construction and use in the 'human garbage' drama, the findings suggest that within the community, although the same categories were often used, they evoked different meanings for different users. When the same categories were employed to describe different things, drama developed because users constantly needed to clarify and make explicit what would otherwise be 'common sense'.

The findings show how users employed devices in the 'locally situated conditions of relevance, activity and context' (Housley & Fitzgerald, 2002:68), meeting the needs of a particular moment in the drama. The conditions of relevance, activity, and context were dynamic, with different users interacting at different times on different pages. How categories were used was never fixed, even conventionalized categories such as 'Christian' or 'fundamentalist'. Although temporary stabilizations could be observed in stretches of discourse on particular video pages (with use, for example, of the category of 'psychopath' in a stabilized way on philhellenes' video entitled 'YouTube's Psychopath:

Yokeup.' (V5)), these stabilizations did not necessarily endure beyond a particular video page.

Categorization devices were not only, therefore, common-sense stocks of knowledge being applied in local use, but also local, specific uses emerging as stable on different timescales. Categories, like metaphorical language, also became a part of the 'repertoire of negotiated resources' (Holmes & Meyerhoff, 1999) drawn as artefacts from the socio-historical context and localized in the 'human garbage' drama. In particular, the category of 'Christian' taken from the shared socio-historical context was appropriated and re-appropriated in user interaction, with the new formulations having different trajectories depending on how users employed it. The meaning of the category, given the instability of its use and its localized character, could not be treated as only an artefact of a user's 'common-sense stock of knowledge' or a label for a fixed group of referents as Sacks' (1995) conception of 'membership categories' do. Instead, the meaning of the category was determined by the purpose it served – most frequently to negatively describe another user.

The dynamic nature of categorization also challenged a notion of categories acting as labels for group membership, as suggested in self-categorization theory (Abrams & Hogg, 2010) and showed instead, how categorization met the needs of a particular discourse context. Because categorizations were 'achievements of members' practical *actions* and practical reasoning' (Hester, 1994:242 cited in Housley and Fitzgerald, 2002, my emphasis), categorizations effected change in the community. Users employed 'types of Christians' categorization devices, for example, to present the offensive actions of individuals as representative category-bound activities of 'Christian'. The actions of the representative 'Christian' were then used to negatively evaluate and reject Christianity more generally as commenters disputed whether a single user could be representative of the 'Christian' category or not, challenged the categorization of others, and asserted their own 'types of Christians' devices. Arguments about 'Christian' categories contributed to the development of drama by giving users a topic of disagreement and conflict. Moreover, when categorization was used to connect the negative action of a single user to a category, drama developed in resistance to the extension of the negative evaluation to others.

The categorization of Yokeup by philhellenes as a 'perfect Christian', for example, was a part of extending a negative evaluation of Yokeup to all Christians, based on Yokeup's actions. In the context of the video page, the categorization was useful in negatively evaluating all Christians, but that did not necessarily mean that the same categorization would be useful in other contexts or for different users. The categorization accomplished a particular action at a particular point with a particular outcome, namely to discredit Yokeup and Christianity, but other users were never grouped together with Yokeup as 'Christians'.

The practical nature of categorization which Hester (1994) highlights also provides some explanation for why denominational categories in particular were not frequently employed to distinguish between users. Because the focus of discourse was consistently on the actions of others, which formal group a user may or may not be a member of was not an explicit topic of disagreement nor a useful way to distinguish between users who, for example, felt that 'human garbage' was an accurate development of Biblical metaphorical language or not. Throughout the 'human garbage' drama, little discussion occurred about what another user believed or how their actions were based on their belief, the focus instead being on what a user had done or should do. Categorization based on denomination (or any other formal institution with formal membership) arguably would not have been relevant for evaluating a particular action.

Categories also evidence the influence of the socio-historical context, instantiated in Crosisborg's attempt to describe Yokeup as 'American white trash'. In this categorization of Yokeup, Crosisborg appealed to a context beyond the 'human garbage' drama to a power structure in which the rural poor are dominated and devalued. By categorizing Yokeup in this way, Crosisborg's attempt at dominance revealed the larger social world in which YouTube was embedded. The power structure of the online world was not separated from the offline world, and users brought the same prejudices and stereotypes from their offline contexts. The use of 'American white trash' revealed that, in this drama, conceptions of larger power structures could influence small-scale internet interaction.

As with the extension of metaphor, the use of categories and category-bound activities from the Bible included an appropriation of the authoritative voice of the Bible. By categorizing users with Biblical language, Yokeup and other Christians were able to re-voice the moral authority of the text. The categorizations were then presented as based on the words of the Bible rather than simply as the opinion of a single user. The use of Biblical categories allowed the user to apply the Biblical text to a particular person or interaction in the community and recontextualize any interaction between users in terms of the 'enduring themes' of the Bible in the same way that Malley's (2004) work showed Evangelical Christians applying the most 'relevant' interpretation of the Bible. The continuous presence of Biblical language and categories in Christian discourse showed the predominance of this practice in the community.

Self-proclaimed 'believers', including Yokeup, christoferL, and commenters on their video pages, used the moral authority of the Bible to support categorizations, deriving categories, category-bound activities, and categorization devices from Biblical language. To highlight the source of the language, Yokeup and christoferL read Biblical passages aloud prior to categorization, presenting their subsequent categorization of others as authoritative. The moral authority of the Bible was applied not only to categories taken from the text of the Bible, such as 'enemy of God' or 'withered branches', but also categories developed from Biblical metaphorical language, including 'human garbage'. Many of the Biblical categories and category-bound activities were also metaphorical and included conventionalized metaphors taken directly from the Bible, such as 'saved' and 'born again', as well as categories taken from specific Biblical parables

Although Christians Yokeup and christoferL appropriated the moral authority of the Bible in categorization and appeared to ostensibly have the same beliefs about the Bible and its interpretation, they still disagreed about categories and the category-bound activities and predicates that should be applied in categorization of others. Their arguments showed that the Christian practice of using certain passages of the Bible to interpret other passages of the Bible can be felt to be done 'wrongly' when a user believes a text has been, as Allington states, taken ' "out of context" (i.e. that the meaning or significance the quoted portion of text bears in context of the interpretation is not one that can reasonably be ascribed to it in context of the text in which it originated)' (Allington, 2007:47). Although Yokeup and christoferL used many of the same categories, how they were used differed despite referencing the same

Biblical passage. The disagreements about how Biblical language should or should not be used in categorization showed again that while the moral authority of the Bible was appropriated in the process of categorization, others who accepted the moral authority of the Bible would not necessarily agree on its appropriation.

Metaphorical language in categorization highlighted the ways in which disagreement in the 'human garbage' drama often led to negative evaluations of other users and their actions. When one user's categorization of another included a negative evaluation, the category was often metaphorical, for example the development of language around mental health illness in escalating negative descriptions of Yokeup. The categorization of Yokeup was also extended and further negative evaluations of him were exaggerated, particularly as users added new category-bound activities and predicates.

Similar to the findings of Fitzgerald, Housley, and Jayyusi (Fitzgerald, 2012; Fitzgerald & Housley, 2007; Jayyusi, 1984) categorization could also imply moral judgements of others; categorization was used to build stereotypes by describing another's action and then applying the action to the category. Rather than presenting an individual as acting in a certain way because they were a member of a certain category, the categorized individual was presented as acting in a certain way and therefore a member of a certain category. If a user categorized Yokeup as a 'Christian' based on his actions, the categorization led to stereotyping of all Christians. If a user worked to distinguish Yokeup from other 'Christians', it implied moral judgement.

In tracking the development of drama in discourse, after describing how categorization occurred and how it led to disagreement, a final step of analysing the action categorization accomplished was needed to understand its role in the 'human garbage' drama. Moreover, although categorization analysis revealed how users spoke about others in the community, users rarely self-categorized. Understanding a speaker's own position therefore requires further analysis to describe how categorization related to positions users took for themselves, what action was accomplished in categorization, and how that action may have contributed to the development of drama. I will return, therefore, to categorization as a part of positioning analysis in the next chapter to further consider these issues.

5

'Friends of the World and Enemies of God': Metaphor in Conflicting Storylines

Having looked closely at the discourse in the drama and analysed how metaphor and categorization played a key role in its development, in this final analysis chapter I would like to take a more comprehensive look at how the drama in these individual interactions developed into a larger struggle between users. Within each interaction in the drama, users were presenting themselves and others as part of different overarching stories about the social world of YouTube. This chapter will explore how these differing positions led to an overarching story of conflict in the community that user narratives followed.

Positioning in social interaction

At the beginning of this book, I suggested that thinking of the YouTube community as a static social grouping would not be useful in describing the complex interaction that occurred within the community I observed. From this conception of the 'community' on YouTube, we have looked at individual instances of interaction, focusing on how users attempted to act on others using metaphor and categories, and effect change in the community. These individual interactions then developed into drama over time, not between different groups of individuals necessarily, but between different storylines about the actions of Yokeup and how users should respond to him. To describe these storylines and investigate how they develop from individual positions that users take, we must take a view of social interaction that takes into account the complex system of interaction of YouTube and how users see themselves in the social space.

In the previous chapter, I discussed how social identity theory (Tajfel, 1981, 1983; Tajfel & Turner, 1979) offers a cognitive conceptualization of group as a product of people's self-perception (Hogg, 2004) of their own identities in relation to others in a community. Hogg describes social identity theory as 'intended to be a social psychological theory of intergroup relations, group processes, and the social self' (Hogg, Terry, & White, 1995:259). The notions of ingroups and outgroups describe how group membership is negotiated not primarily as a product of interaction, but as an abstract cognitive representation that is constructed through practice (Abrams, 1996; Holmes & Meyerhoff, 1999). Notions of grouping that developed in tandem with the theory were also cognitive (Brewer, 1979) and supported by empirical evidence that introducing concepts of 'groups' in experimental settings affected the behaviour of research participants (Billig & Tajfel, 1973) particularly as they related to intergroup preference (Sherif, 1988). In social identity theory, how people perceive themselves is central to how they talk and think about group membership.

The drama I have so far analysed in this book thus far challenges, in some ways, the notions of 'ingroups' and 'outgroups'. Over the course of the drama, whom users affiliated with changed over time and delineating different groups would be difficult. When Yokeup and Crosisborg argued, for example, they did so as individuals appealing to other users to support them, not as members of different groups. The social interaction was oriented towards different disagreements that occurred in the community, giving users the opportunity to develop their own identities and positions in response to the words and actions of others. Rather than form groups of affiliated users, each video and response was an opportunity to present one's own understanding of the world in relation to others. I have highlighted how user discourse in particular instances worked to appeal to diverse sets of users. Analysis of the interaction in the drama may then benefit from looking beyond ingroups and outgroups.

Proposed by social psychologists Harré, Davies, and van Langenhove, positioning theory describes 'the discursive construction of personal stories that make a person's actions intelligible and relatively determinate as social acts' (Harré & van Langenhove, 1998:16). The concept of a 'position' offers an 'immanentist replacement for a clutch of transcendentalist concepts like "role"', highlighting the 'temporal, transient identities' speakers take in conversation

(Davies & Harré, 1990:45). Rather than viewing social behaviour as a response to social 'stimulus', positioning is 'concerned with revealing the explicit and implicit patterns of reasoning that are realized in the ways that people act towards others' (Harré, Moghaddam, Cairnie, Rothbart, & Sabat, 2009:5–6). Positions are emergent, dynamic, and subject to the context of interaction.

Harré and van Langenhove (1998) describe the structure of interaction as 'tri-polar' with mutually determinate positions, social speech acts, and storylines. How a speaker positions themselves or others in a storyline can either arise naturally in conversation, or from one speaker taking a dominant position in the conversation and forcing others into positions they would not have taken for themselves. Placing oneself and others in a moral space using storylines is 'first-order' positioning and can either be explicit, as in the use of categories, or tacit, in which the storyline implies a position that is not explicitly stated (Sabat, 2003). Harré and van Langenhove (1998:20) offer the example of a person, Jones, telling another person, Smith, 'Please, iron my shirts.' In the utterance, Jones is positioned as someone with the authority to ask Smith to iron the shirts, and Smith is positioned as one who serves Jones. 'Second order' positioning occurs when a position is contested within a conversation and negotiation of positions results. What storyline emerges will depend on how Jones responds to Smith, if Jones contests the position or repositions in response to Smith. When the negotiation of a position occurs outside of the conversation where the initial position was established, 'third order' positioning is said to occur.

Positioning is said to be malignant when it has a negative effect not only on the person positioned, but on the ways in which a person is subsequently treated by others (Sabat, 2003). Key to malignant positioning is the deletion of certain rights of the positioned individual (Harré & Van Langenhove, 2008). In Sabat's work investigating talk about patients suffering from Alzheimer's disease, for example, malignant positioning resulted in patients' rights, such as the right to be heard, being deleted as doctors and caretakers spoke about them (Sabat, 2001). In Sabat's analysis, examples of malignant positioning were both explicit and implicit. Explicit malignant positioning occurred when a clear statement about the patient was made, as in, 'They don't know anything anymore' (Sabat, 2003:87). Implicit positioning occurred when caretakers and doctors spoke about being 'amazed' at the way patients spoke about their own forgetfulness. As the action was presented as not meeting the expectations of doctors, an implied positioning of patients as being unwilling or unable to speak about their own illness was accomplished.

Identification of implicit positioning as well as whether positioning is 'intentional' or 'tacit' (a distinction made by Harré and van Langenhove) can be difficult to deduce. Although 'intent' may be ultimately impossible to recover, evidence of perception of intent is potentially observable in the discourse. As Sabat's analysis shows, identifying the positioning of others can involve recognizing potential expectations of speakers, revealed not only in what people say, but in what they do not say, as well as in the talk that immediately precedes and follows a potential positioning. Moreover, storylines can reveal implicit malignant positioning. Again, in Sabat's (2003) data, patients' repetitive actions were described as 'non-physically aggressive' after a series of treatments. The evaluation of actions within a storyline of treatment, therefore, revealed a malignant positioning of patients as generally acting in an aggressive manner.

In terms of the 'human garbage' drama, positioning analysis provides a useful final step, allowing us to talk not only about the nuts and bolts of the discourse in the drama, but to put together the information so far gleaned from analysis and talk not only about instances of disagreement in the videos, but more broadly about how users portrayed the social world, and their own positions within it, in differing and conflicting ways over time. Using positioning analysis, particular interactions can be isolated and analysed for the particular work done by the interactants, but by looking at the larger trends in storylines, a fuller picture of the social world the users created can be seen.

Doing positioning analysis

Harré and colleagues (2009:9) describe the work of the positioning analyst as 'display[ing] the positions that seem to have been immanent in an interaction in a description of the norms'. Positioning analysis has been employed in descriptions of conflict to uncover symmetrical storylines told by opponents, by displaying how people 'define and allocate positions for their rivals' (Harré et al., 2009:9). Because positions are not static 'roles', the positioning analyst takes into account how positions shift over time, including within individual instances of talk or text. Positions are dynamic, but can also be stable over time, or shift gradually or immediately, depending on the context of any given stretch of talk or the social situation.

Analysis of positioning can also be used to see how individuals take similar positions in different contexts. For example, in Jones' (2006) analysis of elderly people's narratives about age categories, interviews were used to produce narratives about ageing. The analyst served as interviewer, prompting particular narrative oriented towards a particular topic, and then used narrative analysis to describe how speakers defined and allocated positions within their talk. The unit of analysis was the narrative from the interview, the analyst interviewed twenty-three individuals and also compared how participants positioned themselves and other 'older people' in their separate narratives, producing an analysis that took into account both individual narratives and how norms emerged across the narratives. In addition to spoken discourse, both Harré's (2000) study of the positions allocated in discourse about terrorism and Sabat's (2003) studies of malignant positioning in talk about Alzheimer's patients included additional texts, such as newspaper articles, speeches, as well as interaction between speakers. By comparing narratives and investigating similarities and differences, a macro-level understanding of how individual narratives relate to a larger social world and how different people talk about the world in different ways could be accomplished.

Building on these methods, I first adapted Jones' (2006) approach to narrative analysis of positioning for the YouTube video page, treating the video talk as the primary unit of analysis. After completing analysis of metaphor and categorization, I began by describing explicit first- and second-order positioning. I began my description of user positions by analysing video talk, building on analysis of categorization because explicit positioning often occurred as a categorization. For example, the categorization of some users as 'the lost' by a Christian was also an explicit positioning of these users. Descriptions of implicit positioning then followed from description of explicit positions, particularly when user positioning of another implied a position for the speaker. For example, whenever a user read aloud from the Bible, they took an implicit position for themselves as a 'scriptural authority', often contrasting with the explicit or implicit positioning of another user as ignorant of the Bible.

Following this analysis, I analysed the effect of user positioning. In Sabat's (2003) definition, 'malignant positioning' has a negative effect on how a person is subsequently treated by others. The effect of malignant positioning can, therefore, be traced by investigating how individuals respond to the positioning of another. Within the YouTube context, responses to positioning can be seen in comments sections and video responses, showing what effect user positioning has on the discourse of others. When, for example, Crosisborg accomplishes a malignant positioning of Yokeup as 'American white trash' in the video entitled 'Yokeup: Poster Boy For Bad Christians' (V3), the negative effect of the positioning can be seen in the comments section when commenters respond by treating Yokeup negatively. When user positioning of another resulted in a negative response, I then described that positioning as malignant. Analysis of malignant positioning added to analysis of impoliteness by providing a description of potential negative effects of, in particular, speaking and acting offensively.

After describing positioning, I then investigated how positions defined and allocated within individual videos followed particular 'storylines'. Because positioning analysis followed from metaphor, categorization, and impoliteness analyses, in constructing potential storylines, I was able to return to the metaphorical stories users told, user text and talk which employed categories derived from the Bible, and negative attitudes towards certain words and/or interactions, in describing how storylines emerged in talk and what moral authority the users accepted. For example, users employed Biblical parables and categories to position themselves and others, establishing the Bible as a moral authority and following storylines derived from the text. After constructing storylines from user talk, I then compared them across the video pages to investigate similarities and differences among users, particularly as they related to the positions users defined and allocated in the interactions.

Because of the centrality of verbal and written communication on video pages and the research focus, aims, and questions, this project foregrounds analysis of text and talk in drama. The vlogs analysed in this research consist primarily of users speaking directly to a camera with the framing of the user's face or body stable over the course of the recording. In several instances, audio from another user's video is extracted and replayed, but no videos include appearances by more than one user. Presentation of self, however, including how a user dresses, where they position the camera, where they shoot the video as well as the tone of their voice and gestures are potentially additional elements that could factor in how a user is perceived by others online and there is evidence that multimodal interactional elements can be fundamentally important to how a particular interaction develops (Cienki, 2010). Taking into account the kind of videos that I analysed, I chose to include the image as part of my analysis of the positioning. I first described how positions were defined and allocated and then returned to the video image to analyse how positioning was embodied in the video image.

Shifting positionings and conflict

Throughout the human garbage drama, the Christian users Yokeup and christoferL explained their own words, actions, and beliefs using the Bible, particularly when replying to negative responses from others. The way that Yokeup spoke of 'preaching love' while claiming that the term 'human garbage' came from the Bible, however, was viewed negatively, and Yokeup attempted to resolve this conflict by shifting positionings which appealed to different users at different times. To illustrate this phenomenon, I now describe Yokeup's attempt to position himself as an 'ally of God' in a storyline of 'war between allies and enemies of God', while also positioning himself as a 'loving preacher' led to disagreement among users about what Christians could say about themselves and others by appealing to the Bible.

Prior to the first videos posted in the 'human garbage' drama, Crosisborg called Yokeup's wife Caroline a lesbian; an insult that was offensive to both Yokeup and Caroline. In many videos posted on Yokeup's channel, Caroline described her conversion to Christianity, a narrative which included the claim that although she was originally a homosexual, she had become a heterosexual after she converted. In her discourse, she positioned herself as a 'wife' in a storyline of 'marriage' with Yokeup. When Crosisborg challenged Caroline's self-positioning, Yokeup initially responded angrily, making an aggressive video that was quickly taken down, but elements of which were remixed and reposted by theoriginalhamster in the video entitled 'yokeup the crackwhore' (V1). The video showed Yokeup angrily calling Crosisborg 'human garbage' and contrasted with the subsequent videos Yokeup posted, in which he claimed that he was only preaching the Bible when he made the first video.

The effect this very personal insult had on the drama was often unspoken in the interaction and Yokeup, rather than referring to the insult being directed at his wife, often condemned other Christians for not helping to protect a 'sister in Christ'. Instead, Yokeup and Caroline's positions as husband and wife were often implicit in their interaction with one another, but not often mobilized in the interaction as a reason for attacking other users. Although discussion did subsequently occur as to whether or not partners and spouses were 'off limits' when attacking another user in drama, because Caroline was also a YouTube user and made her own videos both on Yokeup's channels and on her own, she engaged in the community as an equal user.

As I have shown in the earlier chapters, Yokeup's justification for 'human garbage' prompted responses from other Christians who used the opportunity to both distance themselves from Yokeup and present a more positive Biblical message. christoferL's video entitled 'John 15 for Dummies – Unbelievers are human garbage?' (V12), in which he took a position of openness towards unbelievers, highlighted attempts made by some Christians to position themselves as 'loving Christians' in contrast to Yokeup. christoferL said:

> I recently saw a video where someone used John 15 to justify calling unbelievers as human garbage. This was sent to me by someone who's not a believer who wanted my opinion of the Bible said about him. At first, I wasn't sure what to say but if you saw this video and how it uses the passage, it's quite convincing, however there is a rather obvious point that has been ignored.

christoferL framed his response to Yokeup as addressing the concerns of someone who was not a 'believer' and who wanted to know what 'the Bible said about him'. By reading aloud from the Bible, christoferL's self-positioning also emphasized that he was presenting the 'real' meaning of the Bible and that Yokeup had 'ignored a rather obvious point', accomplishing a tacit malignant positioning of Yokeup as a Christian who 'had gone his own way'. Since Yokeup had claimed the right to call others 'garbage' from the moral authority of the Bible, challenging Yokeup's ability to interpret the Bible also challenged Yokeup's position as a 'loving preacher'. If the moral authority to call others 'garbage' came from the Bible and Yokeup's reading of the Bible was wrong, then his words were not acceptable.

christoferL, on the other hand, maintained a position of a 'loving Christian' by both following the Bible and being open to others. christoferL's response followed a storyline of 'sharing the good news' derived from the Bible, in which 'believers' were, unlike Yokeup, open and friendly, offering the love of God to others without any malice or aggression. christoferL emphasized the theme of openness and concern, tagging the video with the word 'love' and reading from John 15:9–17, which includes nine references to 'love'. In this position, he offered an alternative to Yokeup's aggressive videos and personality. At the same time, however, christoferL asserted that he believed in a literal understanding of hell and was not afraid to tell unbelievers the 'truth' about the Bible. Throughout their interactions, Yokeup had positioned christoferL as a 'weak Christian'(or 'fluffy' Christian) who was quick to avoid unpopular parts of the Bible. In his response to Yokeup, however, christoferL rejected this positioning by stressing that unbelievers will still 'burn' and positioning himself as a 'strong Christian' as well as a 'loving Christian'. christoferL's response to Yokeup did not, therefore, represent a belief that was fundamentally different from Yokeup, and positive responses in the comments showed that many Christians accepted christoferL's self-positioning and saw the two positions as complementary rather than conflicting.

christoferL's physical presentation in videos also reinforced his positioning as a loving Christian. His response to Yokeup was shot while seated and apparently reading from notes he made, including a passage of the Bible. He spoke directly into the camera, and did not frame the image above or below his line of sight, emphasizing a position of equality with the hearer, and contrasting with Yokeup's first video in which he was standing and speaking aggressively at the camera. christoferL's presence instead suggested careful planning and preparation, with an even, measured way of speaking. christoferL continued to assert his own position was not a weak one, but rather came from considering the scripture and responding based on it.

In Yokeup's video entitled 'more on…human garbage' (V14), posted two days after christoferL's video, Yokeup used metaphorical language to position Christians with whom he disagreed as 'enemies of God' in a storyline of 'war between allies and enemies of God' in which every person was either allied with God or God's enemy. Yokeup positioned 'people like christoferL' as 'friends of the world' using the same category-bound activities of 'friends of the world', 'enemies of God', 'unbelievers', and 'human garbage'. This implicit positioning of christoferL as an 'enemy of God' rejected christoferL's self-positioning as a 'loving Christian' and described christoferL's interaction with atheists as befriending people opposed to the moral authority of God. In the storyline of 'war between allies and enemies of God', because 'friends of the world' and 'enemies of God' were destroyed by God in the same way, there was no difference between the positions of christoferL and the unbelievers.

The storyline of 'war between allies and enemies of God' also made sense of Yokeup's treatment of 'hate' from others as something positive because it described interaction between opposing users as part of a struggle between 'good' and 'evil'. Yokeup again presented himself as fervently aligned with God and God's word, and, therefore, more pious than other Christians in the community, particularly christoferL. Throughout his video, Yokeup first read aloud from the Bible before sharing his own opinion, positioning himself and his words as following from the parable of the vine and branches (John 15) as well as James 4 (which explicitly referred to 'friendship with the world' and 'enmity with God') to establish the authority of his words. By explicitly imploring users to '[not] believe anything I'm telling you right now about scripture until you check it out for yourself', he reinforced his self-positioning as Biblical, again affirming his right to call others 'garbage'. By taking this position for himself, Yokeup offered explanations for the criticism he received: he was being hated by the 'world' for following God's word.

Although Crosisborg was not mentioned directly in Yokeup's video, Yokeup's self-positioning within a storyline of 'war between allies and enemies of God' also provided justification for his initial use of 'human garbage'. It was not an insult, but a response to an attack from an 'enemy of God' on another 'ally of God': Caroline. Any resistance from Christians to his use of the term could also then be described as a lack of courage by Christians attempting to be friends of the 'world' (i.e. Crosisborg) rather than fighting for God and God's word. Instead of changing his words, negative evaluations by others served as a further impetus for Yokeup to continue to behave in a similar way. Any attacks on his face were then proof that he was acting in alignment with God.

Some Christians affirmed Yokeup's self-positioning and his right to call others 'human garbage'. As in christoferL's videos, commenters accepted the storyline of 'war between allies and enemies of God' that Yokeup's talk constructed and the malignant positioning of christoferL as an 'enemy of God'. Christian user mackiemoo's verbal threats towards christoferL showed that Yokeup's positioning of christoferL was taken as malignant, and she also evaluated christoferL's actions negatively and responded aggressively towards him. Commenters also followed the same conventionalized Christian narrative and a storyline of 'war between allies and enemies of God' in which only two positions were allocated, 'allies of God' and 'enemies of God', accepting Yokeup's positioning of some self-proclaimed Christians as 'enemies of God'. No commenters challenged Yokeup's positioning of others and his use of 'garbage', and no commenters challenged Yokeup's right to position others, although this apparently reflected Yokeup's moderation of the comments.

Although Yokeup positioned himself as being in a 'war', he also positioned himself as a 'loving preacher'. While positioning others as 'enemies of God' and calling them 'garbage', Yokeup also attempted to present himself as friendly and non-aggressive. At the beginning of 'more on...human garbage' (V14), Yokeup talked happily about the 'beautiful' sunrise, laughing and smiling frequently in the video while speaking in a friendly way. Although he implied that others were 'enemies of God' and said, 'You burn—you're garbage, that's just God's word', Yokeup again insisted his words were simply part of an Evangelical outreach motivated by concern for others rather than misanthropy, saying, 'God bless you guys ... Enjoy your day. That is one beautiful sunrise coming up ... God bless you. Jesus loves you. He has a great plan for your life. If you haven't surrendered to him it'd be the best decision you ever made in your life.'

Yokeup presented himself as showing concern for the viewer, drawing an implicit contrast to positioning of him as a misanthropic person who wanted others to be burned. By asserting that '[Jesus] has a great plan for your life', Yokeup again highlighted the conventionalized Christian narrative in which individuals can be saved from being burned by God's love. Yokeup positioned himself in a manner similar to christoferL, saying 'Jesus loves you' and following a narrative in which Jesus forgives everyone who 'surrenders' to him. The term 'surrender' suggested that, for Yokeup, the positions of an 'ally of God' and 'loving preacher' did not conflict in the 'war between allies and enemies of God' storyline because 'enemies of God' could become 'allies of God' through conversion. In this storyline, attacking 'enemies of God' and 'sharing the love' were complementary, not conflicting.

Yokeup's physical presence reinforced his positioning in the video as a 'loving preacher' in response to Crosisborg and challenged philhellenes' positioning of him as an aggressive, violent person. By framing the video as though he were chatting with a friend in an informal way, Yokeup presented himself as a non-threatening person who was simply and honestly 'sharing the love'. Standing in the front garden of his house, with the sun rising behind him, the natural surrounding was bright, and Yokeup used the setting as a resource for positive self-positioning, remarking about the sunrise, 'My daddy painted that'. Referring to the beautiful natural setting and calling God 'daddy' implicitly challenged negative descriptions of Yokeup and emphasized his childlike appreciation for God and the natural world. Further, by presenting himself in his workout clothing with a hand towel around his shoulders and backwards baseball cap with the words 'Jesus Rocks' written on it, Yokeup reinforced the casual position of a friend talking intimately with another friend. The visual content reinforced the message that the video was not an attack, rather a simple and frank repetition of what the Bible said.

Although Yokeup emphasized this self-positioning as a 'loving preacher', it was not entirely effective and users continued to respond negatively to Yokeup's Evangelical outreach and presence on YouTube. Yokeup's use of 'human garbage' as well as his continued aggression towards others appeared to affect his ability to take the position of a 'loving preacher'. Yokeup's attempts to reposition himself in response to others contributed to the development of drama because each positioning was also an attempt to resolve words and beliefs others in the community saw as conflicting with each other. Yokeup continued to speak in a way that others viewed negatively and continued to argue that his words were acceptable because they were taken from the Bible without ever apologizing for the offence he had caused.

Both christoferL and Yokeup's discourse revealed that, within the 'human garbage' drama, their positions shifted according to the audience they were addressing. Although both users appeared to hold a similar belief in a conventionalized Christian narrative and the moral authority of the Bible, drama developed around whether or not the other saw their beliefs and words as compatible with the Bible. Where disagreement occurred about the rightness of what Yokeup had said, here he positioned himself based on the reactions of others, but never admitted that what he had done or said in the past was wrong.

In this disagreement, a larger struggle developed around how Evangelical users positioned themselves when they presented the 'truth' of the Bible; namely, the unpopular belief that non-Christians would be sent to a literal hell. Even Yokeup, while arguing that enemies of God were 'garbage', attempted to do so in a way that highlighted his own stated concern for others. All Christians in the dataset, regardless of their particular stated beliefs, appeared to consistently position themselves as caring, loving individuals, balancing what they said was the 'truth' of the gospel, with a message of love and acceptance. Although the incongruity of this message was highlighted in Yokeup's attempts to both insist that he loved the viewer even though they were garbage, christoferL's discourse also faced a similar struggle.

Atheists who responded to Yokeup followed a storyline that positioned him as an aggressive, unstable member of the community who attacked and bullied others. Crosisborg, philhellenes, and PaulsEgo not only rejected Yokeup's positioning of himself, but the moral authority of the Bible, and the storyline of 'war between allies and enemies of God'. These users focused on Yokeup's use of the Bible to justify his actions, and positioned themselves as protectors of the community by opposing Yokeup. To illustrate this response, I describe how the atheists rejected Yokeup's calling others 'garbage' and show how they accomplished malignant positionings that undermined his right to call others 'garbage', drawing on response videos posted immediately after Yokeup's first use of 'human garbage' (14–16 January 2009).

Responding to the insult of 'human garbage' in the video entitled 'Yokeup: Poster Boy For Bad Christians' (V3), Crosisborg responded to Yokeup by positioning him as a 'bully' who was acting aggressively towards others in the community. In previous chapters, I have analysed in depth the insults that Crosisborg directed at Yokeup, which described him as attacking others without caring about the consequences. To further highlight the negative response Yokeup had received from both Christians and non-Christians, Crosisborg also reported that the Christian christoferL had rejected Yokeup's words and was likely to have told Yokeup that he was 'not supposed to judge people'. By re-voicing christoferL's words, Crosisborg positioned Yokeup as acting so inappropriately that even other Christians rejected him. This malignant positioning limited Yokeup's ability to be heard in the community by encouraging Christians (to whom Yokeup had appealed by explaining his actions using John 15) to view him negatively, and to oppose him.

Crosisborg also described the interaction among users in terms of struggle, but in contrast to Yokeup's storyline of 'war between allies and enemies of God', Crosisborg described Yokeup as one individual user 'harassing' others rather than a 'war' between Christians and atheists on YouTube. In this storyline, Yokeup was simply a 'bully' and Crosisborg was standing up to him. By taking this position, Crosisborg claimed the right to also act aggressively, since he was responding to Yokeup's violence. The storyline not only provided justification for insulting others, but a moral imperative for Crosisborg to act because the safety of the community was in jeopardy.

Crosisborg's use of the YouTube image also reinforced these positionings. By placing the camera below him, with only his head and shoulders showing, he spoke aggressively about and towards Yokeup. The lighting of the video produced dark edges, emphasizing Crosisborg's aggressive tone. Crosisborg stood and talked down to the camera, accentuating the effect of a superior physical position. Crosisborg also maintained an aggressive and mocking tone throughout the video, addressing Yokeup directly and using his physical stance to reinforce the storyline of Crosisborg standing up to a 'bully'.

Crosisborg's self-positioning as someone protecting others from Yokeup allowed him to describe his actions as both opposed to Christianity in general, but friendly towards Christians whom Yokeup had mistreated. In the 'bullying' storyline, atheists and Christians were not necessarily positioned as opposing groups; instead, Yokeup alone was the 'bully' whose actions had a negative effect on the whole community. By describing Yokeup as attacking everyone regardless of whether they were Christians or atheists, Crosisborg accomplished a more effective malignant positioning of Yokeup, one in which both Christians and atheists viewed him negatively and exerted social pressure on him to stop. By identifying Yokeup's 'bad behaviour' as directed towards Christians, Crosisborg maintained a position that appealed to all users.

Descriptions of Yokeup attacking others within the community were recurring in video responses to his use of 'human garbage'. Both philhellenes and PaulsEgo followed a storyline of 'bullying', and as I have shown in previous chapters, philhellenes and PaulsEgo also rejected Yokeup's attempt to appropriate the Bible's power and to claim the right to speak as he had. Both philhellenes in the video entitled 'YouTube's Psychopath: Yokeup.' (V5) and PaulsEgo in the video entitled 'A spotlight.' (V6) accomplished a further malignant positioning of Yokeup in which Yokeup, as a Christian, accepted the Bible as an authority without question and used the words of the Bible as a justification for violent and hateful words. philhellenes juxtaposed Yokeup's own words that he was 'sharing the truth' and 'sharing the love' from the Bible with audio extracts of Yokeup calling others 'human garbage dumps', implicitly comparing Yokeup to Hitler by suggesting that Yokeup's words reminded him of concentration camps. In describing Yokeup as a potentially violent, psychopathic Christian, philhellenes took the same position as Crosisborg – that of someone protecting others from violence. Illustrated in the *Titanic* story, philhellenes positioned himself in a dominant way, standing between helpless victims and Yokeup. He presented his aggression towards Yokeup as justified because it was only a reaction to others' suffering.

These positions meant that Christians and atheists were not presented as separate groups in the community, struggling against each other, but rather as users struggling against the 'bully', Yokeup. This position made him dangerous and a threat to everyone with whom he interacted, but other Christians in the community were not positioned as 'bullies'. Although at times, negative evaluations of Yokeup were extended to 'Christianity', these evaluations were used to reject Yokeup and Christian doctrine, not reject other self-proclaimed Christians or 'believers'. Throughout the 'human garbage' drama, Yokeup was described negatively, but no specific users were grouped with Yokeup. When self-proclaimed Christians were mentioned, for example, in Crosisborg's talk, they were distinguished from Yokeup and presented as members of the community, not as members of a Christian 'outgroup' in contrast to an atheist 'ingroup'.

In the final atheist response to Yokeup, PaulsEgo followed the same storyline as Crosisborg and philhellenes: that Christians like Yokeup and the Westboro Baptist Church position themselves to be friendly and kind people, but act hatefully and use the Bible to justify their hateful language. PaulsEgo elaborated the storyline, claiming that, 'The problem is that if you dig through that fluff what you find is basically... this beating heart of Christianity that's made of one hundred percent unadulterated hate'. The moral imperative to act strongly against Yokeup was taken, not from a comparison to a historical narrative (like the *Titanic* or the Holocaust), but to the contemporary example of the Westboro Baptist Church. By using an example of a group that was well known for hate, PaulsEgo made a clear moral argument for attacking and stopping Yokeup. Although Crosisborg and philhellenes' malignant positioning of Yokeup attempted to silence Yokeup, PaulsEgo suggested a different tactic. He stated that he hoped Yokeup's 'entire channel becomes this hate filled fuckin' bile' as this would continue to illustrate what he claimed to be the 'beating heart of Christianity'. This malignant positioning, therefore, did not attempt to deny Yokeup the right to speak, but rather the right to determine the meaning of his own words and position himself.

Discussion

Given the drama that developed, it is not surprising that users had different opinions about each other's actions. Users evaluated the positioning of others in conflicting ways, with one user describing an action (such as evangelizing other users) as 'good', while another described the same action as 'bad'. The evaluation of what others said and did was unpredictable and did not depend on whether a user was a Christian or not, or whether or not the users shared the same positioning. Christian users who shared the same self-categorizations still disagreed about which words and actions were 'good' or 'bad', despite a shared belief in the moral authority of God and the Bible. Because users evaluated the actions of others in conflicting ways, drama developed in disagreements over what constituted 'good' words and actions.

Users took varying positions to appeal to different users at different times within videos and at different points in the drama. This variability in positioning was often the result of attempting to appeal to many different users. Because videos often addressed more than one person or topic, how users positioned themselves and others could shift over time or within a single video. One outcome of these shifting positionings was that distinct groups of Christians and atheists did not emerge in interaction. Instead, user positioning changed in responses to the individual contextual circumstances rather than emerging as ingroup/outgroup identities.

Because positioning was dynamic and depended on the immediate context, users could not necessarily expect to be supported by others who had supported them in the past or who shared the same belief. Christians in particular did not always agree with one another, and shifting positionings allowed both self-proclaimed Christians and self-proclaimed atheists to appeal to any user to support them, regardless of how the user being appealed to self-identified. This was a predominant characteristic of interaction and appeared to lead to conflict because the question of who would support whom was not stable and conflict could occur among anyone in the community, including among users who had supported one another in previous conflicts.

Malignant positioning was frequent in the drama and contributed to the development of drama when it was extended by users repeating and/or developing negative categorizations and when users subsequently resisted malignant positioning and attempted to convince others in the community to view them positively. Drama continued to develop when users struggled back and forth, each attempting to influence how the other was viewed, and drama between users only ended when one user stopped responding to the other.

In Chapter 4, I described and analysed categorization in the drama, but also showed that users very rarely used categories to describe themselves. An additional step of analysis was therefore needed to describe how categorization of others related to a user's own positioning and how these positionings interacted. Categorization and positioning analysis complemented one another by first revealing explicit positioning of others (in categorization) and showing how those categorizations affected the positions available to the user who was categorized, the speaker, and others (in positioning). Positionings were often accomplished with categorizations, but more than one category could be used to accomplish a single positioning (such as 'friend of the world' and 'enemy of God'), and comparison between the predicates of the two categories further elucidated the positioning. In this way, the two analytic frameworks provided a fuller description of both the development of categories and the action they accomplished.

The storylines revealed in analysis reflect the findings about metaphorical stories showing how users engaged in *allegoresis* (Gibbs, 2011). While metaphorical stories connected interaction in the drama to specific parables or tragic historical narratives, storylines described interaction in terms of larger, non-specific socio-historical themes such as war. In both metaphorical stories and storylines, users described interaction as a struggle between 'good' and 'evil', in a manner similar to Harré's (2000) observations about contrasting accounts from al-Qaeda and the US administration in discourse about terrorism. The storylines that users followed also showed striking contrast in the way in which users described the same actions. The ongoing drama, and the positions that users took within it, suggested that disagreement went beyond whether or not calling another person 'human garbage' was offensive or not. Conflicting storylines and ways of talking about interaction with others evidenced differences in beliefs and expectations that users held about the world, and the conflicting moral imperatives that both felt they had to act in a way that others viewed negatively.

This conflict between Yokeup and the atheists, and the differences in beliefs and expectations that it reveals, might be understood as a microcosm of a larger conflict between so-called 'New Atheism' and Evangelical Christianity. With both attempting to get the last word in the argument, books by atheist authors and scholars like Dawkins' *The God Delusion* (2006) and Harris' *The End of Faith* (2004) are met with Evangelical author responses: *Deluded by Dawkins? A Christian Response to the God Delusion* (Wilson, 2007) and *The End of Reason: A Response to New Atheists* (Zacharias, 2008). This analysis has shown, however, that disagreement stemming from conflicting beliefs and expectations need not be limited to theological or philosophical arguments, but can also include disagreements about social interaction in particular communities. In these disagreements, the global, historical difficulties of interreligious dialogue (often tied to differences in cultural and socio-political identities) are now also present on the internet and social media (Kluver et al., 2008; Selvan, 2003). The site for the disagreement and the way in which it is done, rather than the disagreement itself, is what is new.

Conflict within the community was also not limited to Christians and atheists, with disagreements among Christians central to the ongoing drama. Different positions and storylines were derived both explicitly and implicitly from the Bible in conflict between Yokeup and christoferL, and both used the Bible to justify positioning both of themselves and others. This positioning evidenced Christian belief about the supremacy of the Bible (Packer, 1978) and the importance of second-order discourses about the Bible in shaping belief about the text (Foucault, 1981, 1982), since the Bible was used to add legitimacy and authority to the positions that users took for themselves from the Bible. The moral authority of the Bible was never questioned by Christians, but the authority *claimed* from the Bible was consistently and constantly questioned. Particularly when malignant positioning based on the Bible's moral authority resulted in impoliteness, Christians responded strongly, attempting to maintain positive views of the Bible and Christianity, while still positioning themselves positively.

Roberts (2006) states that communities of practice represent a social configuration that reflects wider social structures and institutions, a description that my findings support. Earlier, I discussed how Crosisborg's use of 'American white trash' showed that the wider social structures in which the users interacted influenced the way users dominated one another. In the same way, by repeating and extending malignant positioning of Yokeup, users showed that some malignant positions do not necessarily require explanation from the speaker and in particular contexts, users can accomplish malignant positioning by employing conventionalized categories from which others infer a negative position or stereotype. Negative categories from the offline world, and the positionings they represent, are, therefore, also present in the online world.

Malignant positioning on single video pages was successful in that the voice of the user positioned could be effectively silenced. While Sabat (2003) notes that individuals can effectively reposition themselves in response to malignant positioning, on YouTube, users can block others on their video pages through moderation of comments and video responses. The individual who has been affected by malignant positioning must either choose to ignore the malignant positioning or respond on their own video page. None of these options, however, allow the user to respond with an equal voice in the context in which they have been positioned. When users responded to malignant positioning by making response videos, drama developed. Malignant positioning of another user was, however, never completely successful given the lack of restrictions in the YouTube platform and because no user could deny another's ability to continue making videos. There was some evidence that negative evaluations of certain users and attempts to dominate them were successful, any user always had recourse to make videos on and moderate their own channel. This did not, however, diminish the effect of malignant positioning of users within the community whose ability to post comments and make videos without negative response was subsequently limited.

The differences in user positioning showed that users within the community had very different perceptions of themselves and their role on the site. While studies into YouTube interaction have described 'YouTube users' or 'YouTubers' (Lorenzo-Dus et al., 2011; van Zoonen et al., 2011), and Lange (2007a) has described YouTube users based on differences in engagement, the dynamics of positioning show that within interaction on YouTube, different contextual factors influence what position a user may take at any given time and these positions lead to different outcomes depending on the context. Because of this complexity, 'typical behaviour' is difficult to define and suggests that credible analysis of users requires observation and analysis of users over time, in a variety of interactions – something that has not historically been a part of YouTube research.

In the first chapter, I considered Herring's (2004) definition of 'community', which focused on identifying certain traits and characteristics in virtual communities, suggesting that a community of practice approach would likely prove more useful in describing interaction in a free, open online environment like YouTube. Analysis in this chapter showed that users did not describe themselves as members of groups, but rather took positions within the community depending on the context. Rather than drama emerging as conflict between pre-existing groups, drama occurred when users positioned themselves and others in conflicting storylines, often in response to others. Although similarities could be observed in the storylines of Yokeup and christoferL, and Crosisborg, philhellenes, and PaulsEgo, Christians did not necessarily group with Christians and atheists with other atheists. User positioning was dynamic and contextual, changing as users appealed to others for support, and these positionings meant that any user could align with anyone else, given the right circumstances.

6

Metaphor in Drama

Given the history of antagonistic interaction within the community, the emergence of drama was not surprising, but the outcome of interaction was not always negative. Near the end of my observation, something quite unexpected occurred. Yokeup and TheAmazingAtheist, arguably two of the most ideologically opposed users on YouTube, made a collaborative video. Both users lived in the Southern US state of Louisiana where, in 2003, Hurricane Katrina had devastated much of the coastal region. TheAmazingAtheist had begun to work with a charity organization in New Orleans to raise money to help rebuild a particularly hard-hit section of the city, the Lower Ninth Ward. As part of this money-raising effort, he held a 24-hour broadcast on the live-streaming video site BlogTV.com, and sought the support of other users, including Yokeup, in raising funds.

On 14 January 2010, one year after the 'human garbage' controversy began, the two met at a truckstop and made collaborative videos in support of the charity. The subsequent dialogue showed the two joking about being the most unpopular atheist and the most unpopular Christian on YouTube, building an affiliation based on their mutual disdain for (and perceived persecution from) the respective 'communities' they are often seen as occupying. Both seemingly put aside the adversarial personas they had cultivated on their channels. Yokeup praised the work that TheAmazingAtheist did to help charity, agreeing that by meeting together, they were 'going beyond labelling' and 'beyond divisiveness' to help one another. Putting aside their differences, both users affirmed that the work of the charity was right and beneficial. By physically 'sitting down together' and speaking face-to-face rather than through a camera, the two presented themselves as united in the shared enterprise of supporting the charity with the shared goal of helping rebuild the place both called home. Yokeup addressed the camera, saying that spiritual battles between the two could be vicious and brutal, but that when they sat down at a table and 'started talking about things,' he was surprised at how much they had in common.

This positive interaction was not isolated and other relationships with a history of conflict could find temporary stability in harmony rather than discord. There were several other anecdotal instances when Christians, despite publicly stating that non-Christians were going to hell, formed friendships with atheists and worked together to produce joint videos. This also occurred between conflicting Christian users, most notably christoferL and Yokeup who, after several years of opposition, reconciled in 2010. The two were eventually able to put aside their differences about each other's behaviour, which they did not always like, and embrace each other as 'brothers'. Indeed, the narrative of conflict was, in most cases, much more intense than the actual conflict between users and it appeared that when given the chance to find common ground and reach past their categorical divides, all users were willing to do so.

Doing discourse analysis of YouTube drama after a period of observation, and undertaking systematic analysis of full video pages with more than one method of discourse analysis provided a rigorous description of one drama event and some insight into how drama develops. Close qualitative analysis of user communication showed how drama emerged from interactions among contextual factors. On the surface, the reasons for drama in a community comprising Christians and atheists with a shared practice of discussing religious issues over the internet seem obviously rooted in different beliefs and worldviews, and the affordances of deindividuation in computer-mediated communication. Analysis has shown, however, that the complexities of this interaction go beyond theology, group membership, and the use of computers. Instead, the 'human garbage' drama emerged from different responses to a particular situated interaction and was sustained by user attempts to create and sustain social spaces that matched their own beliefs about how the world should be.

In the case of the 'human garbage' drama, Yokeup played a central figure in the community in driving the disagreement between users. Yokeup's response to Crosisborg in the first instance started the drama, and his insistence on using the Bible to support himself fuelled the drama as it went forward. Without Yokeup, this particular drama would not have occurred. That said, without the involvement of popular atheist users like philhellenes and PaulsEgo, the reach of the drama might also have been more limited. There was, however, no simple, one reason for the argument. The complex interaction of the various users drawing on different knowledge about the history of the community and what users knew about one another led to the emergence of the particular drama event.

The 'human garbage' drama has shown that metaphor can be used to develop ideas and positions both in opposition to and in support of others through shared metaphor use and metaphor shifting. Metaphor use both shaped, and was shaped by, the social interaction among users. While Cameron's (2010b) work showed how metaphor appropriation and development became an important component of conciliation discourse, this research has shown how metaphor use in interaction can also lead to incitement and antagonism in ongoing conflict. Metaphor use describing others as 'garbage' and 'trash' increased distance among users who opposed each other, with insults being repeated and extended when metaphors were developed. Metaphor allowed users to creatively engage in negative descriptions of others and escalate negative evaluations, often in relation to larger narratives both from the Bible and tragic historical events like the Holocaust.

When users told metaphorical stories, they did so in creative and unexpected ways that evidenced not only a simple mapping of the one concept onto another in an 'idealised cognitive model' (Lakoff, 1987) or a blended cognitive space (Crisp, 2008), but an acute awareness of others' talk. Metaphorical stories and language drawn from the Bible and the socio-historical context became temporary resources in the community. These stories could be stable for specific stretches of text or talk, or could endure for months, depending on how they were employed. Users did not simply repeat the stories of others – they wove the stories into their own narratives. philhellenes took the burning of branches from John 15 and the story of the *Titanic* and created his own narrative that cast Yokeup as the enemy and philhellenes as the hero. In a vivid way, this use of metaphor not only expressed philhellenes' own attitude towards Yokeup, but enabled and provoked responses in which others extended and elaborated his story to present their own attitudes and values. The conflict of these values, embedded in arguments and extensions of stories, contributed to the 'human garbage' drama.

Throughout this book, I have employed terms – 'metaphorical stories', 'systematic metaphor', and 'parable' – to describe systematicity in metaphor use in the data. The emergent, dynamic nature of metaphor use in the videos, however, showed the difficulty in applying these terms definitively to describe what occurred when metaphor was taken from Biblical metaphorical language and animated in discourse. Supporting a key assumption of the discourse dynamics approach, which treats metaphor as a 'temporary stability emerging from the activity of interconnecting systems of socially-situated language use and cognitive activity' (Cameron et al., 2009:64), the findings suggest that although different kinds of systematicity in metaphor use may be theoretically distinguishable, in real discourse, the distinctions are blurred. Gibbs' (2011) description of the allegorical impulse – allegoresis – was a useful starting point, but actual metaphor use around the connection of immediate context to enduring themes occurred in diverse, interdependent ways.

Findings also showed how metaphorical language from the Bible permeated discourse as users attempted to appropriate its moral authority. In re-voicing and extension, the 'word of God' was not only the actual (or literal) words of the Bible, but the extension of metaphors taken from the Bible. Second-order discourses and pastoral power, like the dogma of the institutional church in Foucault's (1981, 1982) work, held the same power as the actual text of the Bible. When users then spoke about the immediate context and the actions of others using Biblical metaphorical language, they attempted to effect change by representing their own desires as those of God – the ultimate authority. When individuals held differing opinions about how Biblical language should be interpreted, a struggle resulted among users to make their own worldview dominant, obscured in arguments about the meaning of metaphors and the Biblical text.

Metaphor was not limited to metaphorical stories. Categorization employing metaphor served as a practical resource to attach negative associations to others and connect the actions of an individual to a category of people. Categories were constructed in discourse using the immediate resources of the context, and in their occasioned use, often led to generalizations that inhibited dialogue among opposing users. When a category of people was condemned on the basis of an individual member, arguments about categories, rather than the rightness or wrongness of their words, developed. In the antagonistic debate, what an individual said mattered less, ultimately, than whether or not what they said and did was considered a characteristic of the category they represented. In this way, categories, like use of the Bible, obscured debate about social interaction in the community and instead encouraged users to take sides in larger arguments about Christian belief or Biblical exegesis.

The dynamic use of categories showed the importance of the immediate context in categorization and challenged the notion of categories and categorization devices as decontextualized and pre-existing apparatuses. Categories did not appear to serve as labels for group membership in the way that self-categorization theory has assumed (Turner, 1985; Turner & Hogg, 1987), but rather were primarily descriptions of individuals and their actions. In this way, categories were given meaning in their use in a particular stretch of text or talk. Even the conventionalized category 'Christian' took on numerous meanings, but it was always tied to an evaluation, in a particular context with a particular purpose: a feature of categorization devices emphasized in the reconsidered model of membership categorization analysis (Hester, 1994; Housley & Fitzgerald, 2002). Denominational categories were rarely used and category-bound predicates were never abstract beliefs or statements of faith. Instead, category-bound activities were what particular people did at particular times, actions that were evidence of the 'sort of things' that Christians do. Categories were filled with meaning, but they had different meanings at different times.

Analysis of categorization provided a detailed, micro-level description of categorization work on video pages. However, how their use was influenced by a broader social context and how the categories were heard and understood by users who were present but did not contribute to the discourse could not necessarily be identified using the tools of categorization analysis. Although categorization analysis allowed for a description of how the category 'American white trash' was developed in discourse, knowledge of the interaction between the socio-historical and local-historical context was essential for understanding the meaning of the term. Here, the 'common sense stocks' of knowledge crucial to Sacks' (1995) membership categorization devices are relevant to understanding how a categorization is accomplished. The empirical evidence in text and talk provided some evidence of inference based on 'common sense', but a full analysis of the use of such categories requires the analyst not only to understand the immediate 'local' discourse context, but also to situate the use in the broader socio-historical context in which the users were interacting – something that was not always immediately clear from the video page.

Users who were categorized in a negative way often responded, attempting to dispute the categorization, resist stereotyping, and discredit the user who had categorized them. When categorizations were rooted in Biblical metaphorical language, drama further developed into arguments about the meaning of the Bible, with Yokeup and christoferL asserting that each other's categorization devices were not authoritative because the Bible had been misread. The discourse continued like the Talmudic arguments analysed in Billig's (1996) work, with both users attempting to get the 'last word'. This too represented a struggle to assert one's own perception of how the world should be, illustrated in how one read the Bible. In the same way that Christians in Malley's (2004) research used their own experience to interpret and apply the text of the Bible, Christians in this data used that text as a resource for describing and understanding the social world, albeit a malleable one shaped by how a user read it and which parts they chose to emphasize.

Antagonism was not the only reason for the 'human garbage' drama. Instead, drama was a complex interaction among different contextual factors, and impoliteness was often part of an expression of disagreement and/or response to others, rather than simply a means of entertainment for users disrupting or 'trolling' the community. As in previous research into YouTube 'flaming' (Lange, 2007a; Moor et al., 2010), interaction that was considered negative by some users was not always viewed negatively by others. Different views depended on individual beliefs and expectations, and a single set of social norms about impoliteness did not emerge. Instead, different user norms and expectations for 'right behaviour' were present alongside one another and frequently led to conflict.

YouTube's technical features also afforded the development of drama by allowing users both to respond quickly to others and to remove their videos if they chose. Users could speak in anger in a retributive response and receive no immediate negative feedback from the individual they were addressing. They could then reformulate their arguments in new videos that were more carefully worded and avoided inflammatory language. The interaction between what the user had said and deleted and the reconstruction of removed videos in discourse meant disagreements occurred not only over what was done and said in the past, but also over how past interactions were remembered and reformulated in the present, as in Edwards' (2008) findings about the recovery of 'intentionality' in past events in police interrogations. The reconstruction and reformulation of the initial insult provided content for drama to continue when users attempted to position themselves and others based on memories and experiences of what had been said and done in the past. The drama on YouTube is consequently not that different from 'drama' offline. The technology simply provides a new affordance for recalling and retelling what has occurred in the past.

This analysis, in the same way as Culpeper's (2011) updated definition of 'impoliteness', downplayed a notion of strategic attack on face, and focused instead on how individuals experienced different situated interaction. Because the community contained many opposing relationships between users with dynamic, 'mutually defining identities' (Holmes & Meyerhoff, 1999), which were conflictual and contrasting, negative responses from opposed users could be seen as signs of 'positive face'. The 'positive face' was not only 'culture-specific' (O'Driscoll, 1996), but, like impoliteness more generally, contextually specific, dependent on who was engaged in the interaction and what their desired response from a particular audience was. Here, my work highlighted Culpeper's (2008) notions of different levels of 'norms' in the conflicts in the community between how users expected social organization and interaction to be, how they wanted it to be, and/or how they thought it ought to be. Users had such different views about what constituted 'right' and 'wrong', and there was little opportunity for social norms, like those observed by Angouri and Tseliga (2010) in other online communites, to emerge. Instead, the expectations and beliefs of users appeared to be in perpetual conflict.

The perpetual conflict did not necessarily have a negative effect on the community. Indeed, the conflict among members served as a constant source for more topics of discussion and more reason to engage with one another. Although some users dropped out of the community after being attacked, on the whole, the central figures in particular continued to engage in and apparently enjoy the antagonistic back and forth of the drama interactions. The users continued to respond to each other and rather than turning off their cameras and walking away, made more videos and came back again and again to respond to each other. If drama was not something users wanted to engage in, they could have easily avoided it. The fact that they sought it out suggested that it was appealing in some way to them.

Because of the nature of this interaction, the definitions of 'face' and 'impoliteness' that I employed throughout the book were, at times, useful in describing interaction, but the complexities of the 'human garbage' drama showed their insufficiencies. In particular, 'face' and 'face-threatening act' did not provide a dynamic enough description of the actual interaction between users, which showed nuance beyond Brown and Levinson's (1987) face dualism and O'Driscoll's (1996) elaboration of 'wants' and 'desires'. Instead, my research found that including both perception and reconstruction of 'intent', my reformulation of the impoliteness forms, taking into account Culpeper's (2011) most recent definition of 'impoliteness', more adequately described how users dynamically perceived and presented their own actions and the actions of others.

Locher's rhetorical claim that 'all impoliteness is about power' (Culpeper, 2008:17) appeared to be true of the 'human garbage' drama. Impoliteness observed in the dataset was often part of an attempt by one user to dominate another. The long history of disagreement in the community, however, meant that offensive words or actions had little effect on changing the content of others' videos and comments. Users instead traded insults back and forth, with each new insult prompting another response. Current offensive words could be linked to what had been said or done in the past and arguments continued as long as users showed interest in the topic, and ongoing conflict became a characteristic of the community.

Positionings of Yokeup by atheist users who responded to him, and vice versa, were crystallized in the storylines followed by the users' discourse and which represented struggles between 'good' and 'evil' in conflicting ways. Although similar in describing their disagreements in terms of violent struggle, users often talked about action (such as evangelizing others) in contrasting ways. One user described his or her own words and/or actions as 'good', while another called the same action 'bad'. As in Harré's (2003) study of the positions allocated in discourse about terrorism, one user's hero was another user's villain; Yokeup's 'sharing the love' was PaulsEgo's 'unadulterated hate'. Storylines evidenced how the socio-historical context of conflict between New Atheism and Evangelical Christianity in which two sides label the other as the true enemy became embedded in the local-historical context of the community.

However, malignant positioning (Sabat, 2003) occurred among all users – even Yokeup and christoferL, two self-proclaimed 'believers' who ostensibly held the same views about the Bible and the social world. Both claimed to believe that the Bible was completely true and trustworthy, and both said explicitly that non-Christians were bound for hell. The difference was then not in beliefs they held, but in how they interacted with others and positioned themselves in the social world. These different positions led to different reactions in the community to their 'preaching the gospel'. As in Lorenzo-Dus and colleagues' (2009) work showing the importance of interactional response in evaluating impoliteness, the ways in which users positioned themselves and in which others responded to that positioning were central to how others subsequently viewed what they had said or done and whether or not a larger disagreement among users emerged.

Positioning frequently did lead to the development of drama because each new controversy provided a new opportunity for users to assert their own beliefs and attitudes from whichever position was the most advantageous. Shifting positionings meant that users did not talk about struggles in terms of fixed ingroup and outgroup membership, but in terms of the immediate drama context. In contrast to a narrative of atheists and Christians fighting over the hearts and minds of people, the community was not simply comprised of groups of atheists and Christians attacking one another. The actual drama was much more nuanced, with users making concessions and taking hard lines in debates depending on whom they were addressing. When it was advantageous, users would take a position in support of someone they had previously opposed, or oppose someone they had previously supported. As in impoliteness, categories, and the meaning of metaphors, contextual factors influenced user positioning.

In positioning analysis, the real value of the discourse dynamics approach to online interaction was evident. By situating the discourse of users in a larger context of interaction, the positions that users took were not analysed as isolated acts on individual pages, but as part of a larger unfolding narrative in the community. Analysis of any individual page included elements that needed to be understood and analysed in the larger context of the interaction among users, particularly when considering how the users were employing different resources that emerged in the community to position themselves. The perspective of observation showed how patterns of positioning related to the immediate needs of the drama context, what words and/or actions user positioning was a response to, and how it affected the overall development of drama.

Given the scope of the book, analysis of the video image was necessarily backgrounded. The moment-to-moment visual representations of the user, their tone of voice, changes in the video image, and user facial expressions and gesture are potentially rich sources of information about social interaction and communication, and the YouTube video page is filled with potential elements for analysis. From close transcription of intonation to network analysis of commenters' interaction over time, more data could further elucidate the dynamics of interaction. Given the scope and constraints in resources, compiling this information was not possible in the timeframe of the project. Although access to users in this study proved impossible, user reports of their intentions and experience of drama might have provided another useful aspect to understanding how drama developed. The study, therefore, also showed that the contentious nature of YouTube drama can make access to users very difficult and that discourse on the video page can provide useful insights about user reports of their own intentions.

Throughout the analysis, the challenges of using YouTube videos as data were apparent. Because of the inevitable fact that some key videos would be removed, potentially important information about how the interaction developed was liable to be lost. The missing videos highlighted the temporal nature of YouTube interaction, in which content is posted and available only for as long as users and/or administrators allow. Indeed, in all the drama I observed on the site, posting and removing videos was a feature of how the site was used. When videos were frequently taken down, the discourse that ensued in their absence, particularly the reconstruction of what a user 'actually meant' or 'intended' in videos that had subsequently been removed, proved to be as significant as the initial video. The study showed that potentially lost data can be recovered in part by analysis of subsequent discourse.

YouTube both brings users closer together and distances them from each other. Although YouTube allows users with vastly different worldviews to suddenly become virtually present in each other's lives, speaking to the camera is not the same as speaking with another human being. The deindividuation of early internet communication thus persists on YouTube, despite improvements in technology and lack of anonymity. Drama highlights this dichotomy: two opposing users are only able to interact because of a technology that also enables their interaction to be more confrontational and argumentative than it might otherwise be if they met face-to-face. Users adopt and adapt the technology both to create meaningful connections they would not otherwise have made in their local context and to perpetuate disagreements with distant 'talking heads'. The technology affords both possibilities and the two are never completely separate from one another.

The empirical study of disagreement among people of different worldviews can help elucidate disagreements, showing where, when, and why discourse becomes contentious and leads to larger conflicts. Instead of only viewing arguments between people of different worldviews on the internet in terms of large issues about differences in theology or philosophy, it is worth learning from the 'human garbage' drama that even big disagreements on the internet can begin as careless insults, heightened by a medium that separates users. When attention is given to how technology shapes the tone and tenor of disagreement, good things can and do happen. Having done the work of analysing this interaction, my desire is for practitioners to take the lessons learned from this research and effect positive change. There is potential in the simple fact that atheists and Christians are speaking to each other on YouTube.

Appendix

Video Page Corpus

V1   **yokeup the crackwhore**
posted 12/1/2009 by theoriginalhamster
1,889 views, 41 comments, 3:32 running time
http://www.youtube.com/watch?v=usEOTu78FC8

V2   **We Can't Choose Our Brothers**
posted 13/1/2009 by christoferL
696 views, 41 comments, 5:18 running time
http://www.youtube.com/watch?v=Wv09vg75iqc

V3   **Yokeup: Poster Boy For Bad Christians**
Posted 14/1/2009 by Crosisborg
2,384 views, 107 comments, 3:31 running time
http://www.youtube.com/watch?v=OpslWW9Vavo

V4   **Human Garbage. . .Are YOU? (My Response)**
Posted 14/1/2009 by dumoktheartist
178 views, 1 comment, 6:59 running time
http://www.youtube.com/watch?v=smyyp07r0mo

V5   **YouTube's Psychopath: Yokeup.**
Posted 14/1/2009 by philhellenes
17,510 views, 613 comments, 10:25 running time
http://www.youtube.com/watch?v=dX5jzMkHL80

V6   **A Spotlight.**
Posted 14/1/2009 by PaulsEgo
13,058 views, 266 comments, 7:05 running time
http://www.youtube.com/watch?v=mEvsCXHmWuw

V7   **I Was Wrong.**
Posted 15/1/2009 by philhellenes
9,037 views, 109 comments, 5:09 running time
http://www.youtube.com/watch?v=oJctXnFJTt4

V8   **Yokeup Reaches New Low (Adult Language)**
Posted 19/1/2009 by Crosisborg
6,581 views, 168 comments, 4:32 running time
http://www.youtube.com/watch?v=cLmNL5QbpYw

V9   **A Message for sistersunshine**
Posted 10/1/2009 by dumoktheartist
340 views, 28 comments, 6:53 running time
http://www.youtube.com/watch?v=vSaeX3GZ0pE

V10   **irrelevant**
posted 9/2/2009 by Yokeup
638 views, 37 comments, 7:34 running time
http://www.youtube.com/watch?v=1DJs141L56k

V11   **are YOU garbage in GOD's eyes?**
posted 13/2/2009 by Yokeup
2,450 views, 67 comments, 7:02 running time
http://www.youtube.com/watch?v=fShrXBWn1tI

V12   **John 15 for Dummies – Unbelievers are human garbage?**
posted 15/2/2009 by christoferL
578 views, 25 comments, 4:54 running time
http://www.youtube.com/watch?v=oAnou0jiOOA

V13   **John 15:1-8 and Human Garbage Part 1**
posted 10/3/2009 by BudManInChrist
293 views, 16 comments, 10:43 running time
http://www.youtube.com/watch?v=YkFlI6vCJEk

V14   **more on. . .human garbage**
posted 17/2/2009 by Yokeup
939 views, 32 comments, 6:03 running time
http://www.youtube.com/watch?v=afgcewnR-uo

V15 **I doubt JezuzFreek is saved . . .**
posted 25/2/2009 by Yokeup
2,426 views, 93 comments, 9:54 running time
http://www.youtube.com/watch?v=cAm5HUfSO4U

V16 **Straight up. . . .Wolves and Garbage. . call it what it is**
Posted 17/3/2009 by Yokeup
524 views, 21 comments, 10:45 running time
http://www.youtube.com/watch?v=EE5FeqjC8s0

V17 **"Human Garbage" – searing TRUTH**
Posted 29/4/2009 by Caroline on the yokedtojesus channel
769 views, 39 comments, 5:31 running time
http://www.youtube.com/watch?v=WVmRr3gstbs

V18 **YokeUp sculpture – confusion on Human Garbage!**
Posted 2/5/2009 by Yokeup
313 views, 14 comments, 9:19 running time
http://www.youtube.com/watch?v=rPoSU6SzKyM

V19 **absolute human Garbage!**
Posted 15/5/2009 by Yokeup
1,403 views, 14 comments, 3:12 running time
http://www.youtube.com/watch?v=DafJbFm9yxQ

V20 **Re: "Human Garbage" – searing TRUTH**
Reposted 9/8/2009 (initial posting May 2009) by gdy50
102 views, 7 comments, 7:21 running time
http://www.youtube.com/watch?v=WFmXbf2AlrU

References

Abrams, D. (1996). Social identity, self as structure and self as process. In W. P. Robinson (Ed.), *Social Groups and Identities: Developing the Legacy of Henri Tajfel* (pp. 143–67). Oxford: Butterworth Heinemann.

Abrams, D., & Hogg, M. (2010). Social identity and self-categorization. In J. Dovidio, M. Hewstone, P. Glick & V. Esses (Eds), *The Sage Handbook of Prejudice, Stereotyping and Discrimination* (pp. 179–93). London: Sage.

Allington, Daniel. (2007). "How come most people don't see it?": Slashing the Lord of the Rings. *Social Semiotics*, *17*(1), 43–62.

Androutsopoulos, J. (2008). Potentials and limitations of discourse-centred online ethnography. *Language@Internet*, *5*. Retrieved from Language@Internet website: http://www.languageatinternet.org/articles/2008/1610

Angouri, Jo, & Tseliga, Theodora. (2010). 'You have no idea what you are talking about!' From e-disagreement to e-impoliteness in two online fora. *Journal of Politeness Research: Language, Behavior, Culture*, *6*(1), 57–82.

Barsalou, L. W. (1999). Perceptual symbol systems. *Behavioral and Brain Sciences*, *22*(4), 577–660.

—— (2008). Grounded cognition. *Annual Review of Psychology*, *59*, 617–45.

Bartkowski, J. (1996). Beyond biblical literalism and inerrancy: Conservative Protestants and the hermeneutic interpretation of scripture. *Sociology of Religion*, *57*(3), 259–72.

Bebbington, D. W., & Bebbington, D. (1989). *Evangelicalism in Modern Britain: A History from the 1730s to the 1980s*. London: Routledge.

Beebe, L. M. (1995). Polite fictions: Instrumental rudeness as pragmatic competence. In James E. Alatis (Ed.), *Linguistics and the Education of Language Teachers: Ethnolinguistic, Psycholinguistic, and Sociolinguistic Aspects* (pp. 154–68). Washington DC: Georgetown University Press.

Bible Gateway. (n.d.). Bible Gateway. Retrieved Various Dates, 2010–12, from http://www.biblegateway.com/

Billig, M. (1996). *Arguing and Thinking*. Cambridge: Cambridge University Press.

Billig, M., & Tajfel, H. (1973). Social categorization and similarity in intergroup behaviour. *European Journal of Social Psychology*, *3*(1), 27–52.

Blood, R. (2004). How blogging software reshapes the online community. *Communications of the ACM*, *47*(12), 53–5.

Bodenhausen, G. V., Mussweiler, T., Gabriel, S., & Moreno, K. N. (2001). Affective influences on stereotyping and intergroup relations. In J. Forgas (Ed.), *Handbook of Affect and Social Cognition* (pp. 319–43). Abingdon, UK: Psychology Press.

Boone, K. C. (1989). *The Bible Tells Them So: The Discourse of Protestant Fundamentalism*. Albany: State University of New York Press.

Bousfield, Derek. (2008). Impoliteness in the struggle for power. In Derek Bousfield & Miram Locher (Eds), *Impoliteness in Language*. Berlin: Mouton de Gruyter.

Bousfield, Derek, & Locher, Miram. (2008). *Impoliteness in Language: Studies on its Interplay with Power in Theory and Practice*. Berlin: Mouton de Gruyter.

Bowdle, B. F., & Gentner, D. (2005). The career of metaphor. *Psychological Review, 112*(1), 193–216.

Brewer, M. B. (1979). In-group bias in the minimal intergroup situation: A cognitive-motivational analysis. *Psychological Bulletin, 86*(2), 307–24.

British Association of Applied Linguistics. (2006). BAAL Research Guidelines. Retrieved from British Association of Applied Linguistics website: http://www.baal.org.uk/dox/goodpractice_full.pdf

British National Corpus. (n.d.). British National Corpus. Retrieved various dates, 2010–12, from http://www.natcorp.ox.ac.uk/

Brown, Penelope, & Levinson, Stephen. (1987). *Politeness: Some Universals in Language Usage*. Cambridge: Cambridge University Press.

Burgess, Jean, & Green, Joshua. (2008, 15–18 October). *Agency and controversy in the YouTube community*. Paper presented at the Internet Research 9.0: Rethinking Community, Rethinking Place, Copenhagen.

Burgess, Jean, & Green, Joshua. (2009). *YouTube: Online Video and Participatory Culture*. Cambridge: Polity Press.

Burke, K. (1945). *A Grammar of Motives*. New York: Prentice Hall.

Cameron, L. (2003). *Metaphor in Educational Research*. London: Continuum.

—— (2008). Metaphor shifting in the dynamics of talk. In M. S. Zanotto, L. Cameron, & M. C. Cavalcanti (Eds), *Confronting Metaphor in Use: An Applied Linguistic Approach* (pp. 45–62). Amsterdam: John Benjamins.

—— (2010a). The discourse dynamics framework for metaphor. In L. Cameron & R. Maslen (Eds), *Metaphor Analysis: Research Practice in Applied Linguistics, Social Sciences and the Humanities* (pp. 77–96). London: Equinox.

—— (2010b). *Metaphor and Reconciliation: The Discourse Dynamics of Empathy in Post-Conflict Conversations*. London: Routledge.

—— (2010c). Metaphors and discourse activity. In L. Cameron & R. Maslen (Eds), *Metaphor Analysis: Research Practice in Applied Linguistics, Social Sciences and the Humanities* (pp. 147–61). London: Equinox.

—— (2010d). What is metaphor and why does it matter? In L. Cameron & R. Maslen (Eds), *Metaphor Analysis: Research Practice in Applied Linguistics, Social Sciences and the Humanities* (pp. 3–25). London: Equinox.

Cameron, L., & Low, G. (1999). *Researching and Applying Metaphor*. Cambridge: Cambridge University Press.

Cameron, L., Low, G., & Maslen, R. (2010). Finding systematicity in metaphor use. In L. Cameron & R. Maslen (Eds), *Metaphor Analysis: Research Practice in Applied Linguistics, Social Sciences and the Humanities*. London: Equinox.

Cameron, L., & Maslen, R. (2010a). Identifying metaphors in discourse data. In L. Cameron & R. Maslen (Eds), *Metaphor Analysis: Research Practice in Applied Linguistics, Social Sciences and the Humanities*. London: Equinox.

—— (2010b). *Metaphor Analysis: Research Practice in Applied Linguistics, Social Sciences and the Humanitiess*. London: Equinox.

Cameron, L., Maslen, R., Maule, J., Stratton, P., & Stanley, N. (2009). The discourse dynamics approach to metaphor and metaphor-led discourse analysis. *Metaphor and Symbol*, 24(2), 63–89.

Chafe, Wallace. (1994). *Discourse, Consciousness, and Time*. Chicago: University of Chicago Press.

Charteris-Black, J. (2005). *Politicians and Rhetoric: The Persuasive Power of Metaphor*. Basingstoke, UK: Palgrave-MacMillan.

—— (2009). Metaphor and political communication. In A. Musolff & Jorg Zinken (Eds), *Metaphor and Discourse*. Basingstoke, UK: Palgrave Macmillan.

Cienki, A. (2010). Multimodal metaphor analysis. In L. Cameron & R. Maslen (Eds), *Metaphor Analysis: Research Practice in Applied Linguistics, Social Sciences and the Humanities*. London: Equinox.

Coopey, J., & Burgoyne, J. (2000). Politics and organizational learning. *Journal of Management Studies*, 37(6), 869–86.

Copyright, Designs and Patents Act 1988, Chapter 48 (1988).

Corpus of Contemporary American English. (n.d.). Corpus of Contemporary American English. Retrieved various dates, 2010–12, from http://corpus.byu.edu/coca/

Cox, A. (2005). What are communities of practice? A comparative review of four seminal works. *Journal of Information Science*, 31(6), 527–40.

Crisp, P. (2008). Allegory: Conceptual metaphor in history. *Language and Literature*, 10(1), 5–19.

Culpeper, Jonathan. (2005). Impoliteness and entertainment in the television quiz show: The Weakest Link. *Journal of Politeness Research. Language, Behaviour, Culture*, 1(1), 35–72.

—— (2008). Reflections on impoliteness, relational work and power. In D. Bousfield & M. A. Locher (Eds), *Impoliteness in Language: Studies on its Interplay with Power in Theory and Practice*. Berlin: Mouton de Gruyter.

—— (2011). *Impoliteness*. Cambridge: Cambridge University Press.

Culpeper, Jonathan, Bousfield, Derek, & Wichmann, Anne. (2003). Impoliteness revisited: With special reference to dynamic and prosodic aspects. *Journal of Pragmatics, 35*(10–11), 1545–79.

Davies, B., & Harré, R. (1990). Positioning: The discursive production of selves. *Journal for the Theory of Social Behaviour, 20*(1), 43–63.

Dawkins, R. (2006). *The God Delusion*. London: Transworld Publishers.

De Laat, M. (2002). *Network and content analysis in an online community discourse*. Paper presented at the Conference on Computer Support for Collaborative Learning: Foundations for a CSCL Community.

Drew, P. (1978). Accusations: The occasioned use of members' knowledge of religious geography in describing events. *Sociology, 12*(1), 1–22.

Dubrovsky, V. J., Kiesler, S., & Sethna, B. N. (1991). The equalization phenomenon: Status effects in computer-mediated and face-to-face decision-making groups. *Human-Computer Interaction, 6*(2), 119–46.

Edwards, Derek. (2008). Intentionality and mens rea in police interrogations: The production of actions as crimes. *Intercultural Pragmatics, 5*(2), 177–99.

Eglin, P. (2002). Members' gendering work: Women, 'feminists' and membership categorization analysis. *Discourse and Society, 13*(6), 819–26.

Eglin, P., & Hester, S. (2003). *The Montreal Massacre: A Story of Membership Categorization Analysis*. Waterloo: Wilfrid Laurier University Press.

Evaldsson, A. C. (2005). Staging insults and mobilizing categorizations in a multiethnic peer group. *Discourse & Society, 16*(6), 763–86.

—— (2007). Accounting for friendship: Moral ordering and category membership in preadolescent girls' relational talk. *Research on Language and Social Interaction, 40*(4), 377–404.

Fernback, J., & Thompson, B. (1995). Virtual communities: Abort, retry, failure? *International Communication Association*. http://www.rheingold.com/texts/techpolitix/VCcivil.html

Fitzgerald, Richard. (2012). Categories, norms and inferences generating entertainment in a daytime talk show. *Discourse, Context & Media*.

Fitzgerald, Richard, & Housley, William. (2007). Talkback, community and the public sphere. *Media International Australia, 122*, 150–63.

Forrester, Duncan. (1981). Biblical interpretation and cultural relativism. In Michael Wadsworth (Ed.), *Ways of Reading the Bible*. Brighton: The Harvester Press Limited.

Foucault, Michel. (1981). The orders of discourse. In Robert Young (Ed.), *Untying the Text: A Post-Structuralist Reader* (pp. 48–78). London: Routledge.

—— (1982). The subject and power. *Critical Inquiry, 8*(4), 777–95.

Frankel, M. S., & Siang, S. (1999). Ethical and legal aspects of human subjects research on the Internet. Retrieved from American Association for the Advancement of Science website: http://www.aaas.org/spp/sfrl/projects/intres/report.pdf

Gentner, D., & Bowdle, B. F. (2001). Convention, form, and figurative language processing. *Metaphor and Symbol, 19*, 223–48.

Gibbs, Raymond. (1994). *The Poetics of Mind: Figurative Thought, Language and Understanding.* Cambridge: Cambridge University Press.

—— (1999). *Intentions in the Experience of Meaning.* Cambridge: Cambridge University Press.

—— (2006). *Embodiment and Cognitive Science.* Cambridge: Cambridge University Press.

—— The Allegorical Impulse. *Metaphor and Symbol, 26*(2), 121–30.

Gibson, J. J. (1979). *The Ecological Approach to Visual Perception.* Boston: Houghton-Mifflin.

Glucksberg, S., & McGlone, M. S. (1999). When love is not a journey: What metaphors mean. *Journal of Pragmatics, 31*(12), 1541–58.

Godwin, Mike. (1994). Meme, counter-meme. *Wired.* Retrieved October 22, 2013, from http://www.wired.com/wired/archive/2.10/godwin.if_pr.html

Goffman, E. (1967). *Interaction Ritual: Essays in Face-to-Face Behavior.* New York: Anchor Books.

Gu, Y. (1990). Politeness phenomena in modern Chinese. *Journal of Pragmatics, 14*(2), 237–57.

Hardaker, C. (2010). Trolling in asynchronous computer-mediated communication: From user discussions to academic definitions. *Journal of Politeness Research: Language, Behaviour, Culture, 6*(2), 215–42.

Harré, R. (2000). The social construction of terrorism. In F. M. Moghaddam & A. J. Marsella (Eds), *Understanding Terrorism.* Washington, D.C.: APA Press.

Harré, R., & Moghaddam, F. M. (2003). *The Self and Others: Positioning Individuals and Groups in Personal, Political, and Cultural Contexts.* Westport, CT: Praeger Publishers.

Harré, R., Moghaddam, F. M., Cairnie, T. P., Rothbart, D., & Sabat, S. R. (2009). Recent advances in positioning theory. *Theory & Psychology, 19*(1), 5–31.

Harré, R., & van Langenhove, L. (1998). *Positioning Theory: Moral Contexts of Intentional Action.* London: Blackwell Publishers.

—— (2008). Positioning theory. *Self-Care & Dependent-Care Nursing, 16*, 28–32.

Harris, S. (2004). *The End of Faith.* New York: W.W. Norton & Co.

Harrison, S. (2000). Maintaining the virtual community: Use of politeness strategies in an email discussion group. In L. Pemberton & S. Shurville (Eds), *Words on the Web: Computer-Mediated Communication* (pp. 69–78). Exeter, UK: Intellect.

Haslam, S. A., & Turner, J. (1992). Context dependent variation in social stereotyping: The relationship between frame of reference, self categorization and accentuation. *European Journal of Social Psychology, 22*(3), 251–77.

Herring, S., Scheidt, L. A., Bonus, S., & Wright, E. (2004). *Bridging the gap: A genre analysis of weblogs.* Paper presented at the Proceedings of the 37th Annual Hawaii International Conference on System Sciences Big Island, Hawaii.

Herring, S. (1996). Linguistic and critical analysis of computer-mediated communication: Some ethical and scholarly considerations. *The Information Society, 12*(2), 153–68.

—— (2004). Computer-mediated discourse analysis: An approach to researching online behavior. In S. A. Barab, R. Kling & J. H. Gray (Eds), *Designing for Virtual Communities in the Service of Learning* (pp. 338–76). Cambridge: Cambridge University Press.

Hester, S. (1994). Les catégories en contexte. *Raisons Pratiques, 5,* 219–43.

Hester, S., & Eglin, P. (1997). *Culture in Action: Studies in Membership Categorization Analysis.* Lanham, Maryland: University Press of America.

Hogg, M. (2004). Social identity theory. In A. H. Eagly, R. M. Baron & V. Hamilton (Eds), *The Social Psychology of Group Identity and Social Conflict: Theory, Application, and Practice* (pp. 111–36): American Psychological Association.

Hogg, M., & Terry, D. (2000). Social identity and self-categorization processes in organizational contexts. *The Academy of Management Review, 25*(1), 121–40.

Hogg, M., Terry, D., & White, K. (1995). A tale of two theories: A critical comparison of identity theory with social identity theory. *Social Psychology Quarterly, 58*(4), 255–69.

Holmes, J., & Meyerhoff, M. (1999). The community of practice: Theories and methodologies in language and gender research. *Language in Society, 28*(02), 173–83.

Hornsey, M. J. (2008). Social identity theory and self-categorization theory: A historical review. *Social and Personality Psychology Compass, 2*(1), 204–22.

Housley, W., & Fitzgerald, R. (2002). The reconsidered model of membership categorization analysis. *Qualitative Research, 2*(1), 59–83.

—— (2009). Membership categorization, culture and norms in action. *Discourse & Society, 20*(3), 345–62.

Ide, S. (1989). Formal forms and discernment: Two neglected aspects of universals of linguistic politeness. *Multilingua-Journal of Cross-Cultural and Interlanguage Communication, 8*(2–3), 223–48.

Jayyusi, L. (1984). *Categorization and the Moral Order.* London: Routledge/Kegan & Paul.

Jones, R. L. (2006). 'Older people' talking as if they are not older people: Positioning theory as an explanation. *Journal of Aging Studies*, *20*(1), 79–91.

Jones, S. (1995). Understanding community in the information age. In S. Jones (Ed.), *Cybersociety: Computer-Mediated Communication and Community* (pp. 10–35). Thousand Oaks, CA: Sage.

Journal of Computer Mediated Communication. (2005). Special Theme: Online Communities. Retrieved August 13, 2012, from http://jcmc.indiana.edu/vol10/issue4/

Kasper, Gabriele. (1990) Linguistic politeness: Current research issues. *Journal of Pragmatics*, *14*, 193–218.

Kiesler, Sara, Siegel, Jane, & McGuire, Timothy. (1984). Social psychological aspects of computer-mediated communication. *American Psychologist*, *39*(10), 1123–34.

King, S. A. (1996). Researching Internet communities: Proposed ethical guidelines for the reporting of results. *The Information Society*, *12*(2), 119–28.

Kittay, E. F. (1987). *Metaphor*. Oxford: Clarendon Press.

Kluver, R., Detenber, B., Lee, W. P., Hameed, S. B. S., Chen, Y., & Cheong, P. H. (2008). The internet and religious harmony in Singapore. In E. Lai (Ed.), *Religious Diversity in Singapore* (pp. 434–56). Singapore: Institute of Policy Studies.

Kollock, P., & Smith, M. (1996). Managing the virtual commons: Cooperation and conflict in computer communities. In S. Herring (Ed.), *Computer-Mediated Communication: Linguistics, Social and Cross-Cultural Perspectives*. Amsterdam: John Benjamins.

Kuiper, K., & Lin, D. T. G. (1989). Cultural congruence and conflict in the acquisition of formulae in a second language. In O. Garcia & R. Otheguy (Eds), *English Across Cultures: Cultures Across English* (pp. 281–304). Berlin: Mouton de Gruyter.

Lakoff, G. (1987). *Women, Fire, and Dangerous Things: What Categories Reveal About the Mind*. Chicago: University of Chicago Press.

Lakoff, G., & Johnson, M. (1980). *Metaphors We Live By*. Chicago: University of Chicago Press.

Lange, Patricia. (2007a). *Commenting on comments: Investigating responses to antagonism on YouTube*. Paper presented at the Society for Applied Anthropology Conference, Tampa, Florida.

—— (2007b). Publicly private and privately public: Social networking on YouTube. *Journal of Computer-Mediated Communication*, *13*(1), 361–80.

Larsen-Freeman, D., & Cameron, L. (2008). *Complex Systems and Applied Linguistics*. Oxford: Oxford University Press.

Lave, J., & Wenger, E. (1991). *Situated Learning: Legitimate Peripheral Participation*. Cambridge: Cambridge University Press.

Lepper, G. (2000). *Categories in Text and Talk*. London: Sage.

Leudar, I., Marsland, V., & Nekvapil, J. (2004). On membership categorization: 'Us', 'them' and 'doing violence' in political discourse. *Discourse & Society, 15*(2–3), 243–66.

Locher, M. (2004). *Power and Politeness in Action: Disagreements in Oral Communication.* Berlin: Mouton de Gruyter.

Lorenzo-Dus, Nuria. (2009). "You're barking mad, I'm out": Impoliteness and broadcast talk. *Journal of Politeness Research: Language, Behaviour, Culture, 5*(2), 159–87.

Lorenzo-Dus, Nuria, Garcés-Conejos Blitvich, Pilar, & Bou-Franch, Patricia. (2011). On-line polylogues and impoliteness: The case of postings sent in response to the Obama Reggaeton YouTube video. *Journal of Pragmatics, 43*(10), 2578–93.

Low, G., & Cameron, L. (1999). *Researching and Applying Metaphor.* Cambridge: Cambridge University Press.

Mailloux, S. (1989). *Rhetorical Power.* Ithaca and London: Cornell University Press.

Malley, B. (2004). *How the Bible Works: An Anthropological Study of Evangelical Biblicism.* Walnut Creek, CA, USA: AltaMira Press.

Mao, L. M. R. (1994). Beyond politeness theory: 'Face' revisited and renewed. *Journal of Pragmatics, 21*(5), 451–86.

Markman, E. M. (1991). *Categorization and Naming in Children: Problems of Induction.* Cambridge, MA: The MIT Press.

Matsumoto, Y. (1988). Reexamination of the universality of face: Politeness phenomena in Japanese. *Journal of Pragmatics, 12*(4), 403–26.

—— (1989). Politeness and conversational universals–observations from Japanese. *Multilingua-Journal of Cross-Cultural and Interlanguage Communication, 8*(2–3), 207–22.

Moor, Peter, Heuvelman, Ard, & Verleur, Ria. (2010). Flaming on YouTube. *Computers in Human Behavior, 26*, 1536–46.

Morris, Sue. (2004). Shoot first, ask questions later: Ethnographic research in an online computer gaming community. *Media International Australia, 110*, 31–41.

Muhr, Thomas (1993–2011). Atlas.TI [computer software]. Berlin: Scientific Software Development GmbH.

Musolff, A. (2004). *Metaphor and Political Discourse: Analogical Reasoning in Debates About Europe.* Basingstoke, UK: Palgrave Macmillan.

—— (2006). Metaphor scenarios in public discourse. *Metaphor and Symbol, 21*(1), 23–38.

Nagata, J. (2001). Beyond theology: Toward an anthropology of "fundamentalism". *American Anthropologist, 103*(2), 481–98.

Nelson, T. D. (2009). *Handbook of Prejudice, Stereotyping, and Discrimination.* Hove, UK: Psychology Press.

Noll, M. A. (2001). *American Evangelical Christianity: An Introduction.* London: Blackwell.

Nuttall, G. F. (1992). *The Holy Spirit in Puritan Faith and Experience*. Chicago: University of Chicago Press.

Nwoye, O. G. (1992). Linguistic politeness and socio-cultural variations of the notion of face. *Journal of Pragmatics, 18*(4), 309–28.

O'Driscoll, J. (1996). About face: A defence and elaboration of universal dualism. *Journal of Pragmatics, 25*(1), 1–32.

Packer, J. I. (1978). *The Evangelical Anglican Identity Problem: An Analysis*. Oxford: Latimer.

Pfannenstiel, A. N. (2010). Digital literacies and academic integrity. *International Journal for Educational Integrity, 6*(2), 41–9.

Pihlaja, S. (2010). The Pope of YouTube: Metaphor and misunderstanding in Atheist-Christian YouTube dialogue. *The Journal of Inter-Religious Dialogue, 3*, 25–35. http://irdialogue.org/journal/issue03/the-pope-of-youtube-metaphor-and-misunderstanding-in-atheist-christian-youtube-dialogue-by-stephen-pihlaja/

—— (2011). Cops, popes, kings, and garbagemen: A case study of dynamic metaphor use in asynchronous Internet communication. *Language@Internet, 8*(1). Retrieved from Language@Internet website: http://www.languageatinternet.de/articles/2011/pihlaja

Pragglejaz group. (2007). MIP: A method for identifying metaphorically used words in discourse. *Metaphor and Symbol, 22*(2), 1–39.

Ray, D. G., Mackie, D. M., Rydell, R. J., & Smith, E. R. (2008). Changing categorization of self can change emotions about outgroups. *Journal of Experimental Social Psychology, 44*(4), 1210–13.

Rheingold, H. (1993; 2000). *The Virtual Community: Homesteading on the Electronic Frontier*. Cambridge, MA: MIT Press.

Ritchie, D. (2003). "ARGUMENT IS WAR" – Or is it a game of chess? Multiple meanings in the analysis of implicit metaphors. *Metaphor and Symbol, 18*(2), 125–46.

—— (2006). *Context and Connection in Metaphor*. Basingstoke, UK: Palgrave Macmillan.

—— (2010). Between mind and language: A journey worth taking. In L. Cameron & L. Maslen (Eds), *Metaphor Analysis: Research Practice in Applied Linguistics, Social Sciences and the Humanities* (pp. 57–76). London: Equinox.

Roberts, J. (2006). Limits to communities of practice. *Journal of Management Studies, 43*(3), 623–39.

Rosch, E. (1973). Natural categories. *Cognitive Psychology, 4*(3), 328–50.

—— (1974). Linguistic relativity. In A. Sliverstein (Ed.), *Human Communication: Theoretical Perspectives*. New York: Halsted Press.

—— (1975). Cognitive representations of semantic categories. *Journal of Experimental Psychology: General, 104*(3), 192–233.

—— (1978). Principles of categorization. In Barbara Bloom Lloyd & E. Rosch (Eds), *Cognition and Categorization* (pp. 27–48). New York: John Wiley and Sons.

Sabat, S. (2001). *The Experience of Alzheimer's*. Oxford: Blackwell.

—— (2003). Malignant positioning and the predicament of people with Alzheimer's disease. In R. Harré & F. M. Moghaddam (Eds), *The Self and Others: Positioning Individuals and Groups in Personal, Political, and Cultural Contexts*. Westport, CT, USA: Praeger.

Sacks, H. (1974). On the analyzability of stories by children. In R. Turner (Ed.), *Ethnomethodology: Selected Readings*. Harmondsworth: Penguin Books.

—— (1995). *Lectures on Conversation*. Oxford: Basil Blackwell.

Schegloff, E. A. (1972). Notes on a conversational practice: Formulating place. In D. N. Sudnow (Ed.), *Studies in Social Interaction* (pp. 75–119). New York: The Free Press.

Schegloff, E. A. (2007). A tutorial on membership categorization. *Journal of Pragmatics*, *39*(3), 462–82.

Selvan, Arul Maragatha Muthu K. S. (2003). Support and spewing: Everyday activities of online Hindu groups. In K. C. Ho, R. Kluver, & K. Yang (Eds), *Asia.com: Asia Encounters the Internet* (pp. 228–48). London: Routledge.

Sherif, M. (1988). *The Robbers Cave Experiment: Intergroup Conflict and Cooperation*. Scranton, PA: Wesleyan University Press.

Siegel, J., Dubrovsky, V., Kiesler, S., & McGuire, T. W. (1986). Group processes in computer-mediated communication. *Organizational Behavior and Human Decision Processes*, *37*(2), 157–87.

souledouttojesus. (2010). Human Garbage? Let's Talk About It. . . Retrieved August 18, 2010, from http://www.youtube.com/watch?v=jvLUkmW3BLU

Southern Baptist Convention. (n.d.). The Baptist Faith and Message. *Southern Baptist Convention Statement of Faith*. Retrieved from Southern Baptist Convention website: http://www.sbc.net/bfm/bfm2000.asp#i

Stanton, J. (2010). YouTube dialogue: Expanding the scope of inter-religious interchange. *Huffington Post: Religion*. Retrieved from The Huffington Post website: http://www. huffingtonpost.com/joshua-stanton/youtube-dialogue-expandin_b_602220.html

Steen, G. (2007). *Finding Metaphor in Grammar and Usage: A Methodological Analysis of Theory and Research*. Amsterdam: John Benjamins.

Stelma, J. H., & Cameron, L. J. (2007). Intonation units in spoken interaction: Developing transcription skills. *Text and Talk*, *27*(3), 361–93.

Tajfel, H. (1970). Experiments in intergroup discrimination. *Scientific American*, *223*(5), 96–102.

—— Social psychology and social reality. *New Society*, *39*, 653–54.

—— (1981). *Human Groups and Social Categories*. Cambridge: Cambridge University Press.

—— (1983). *Social Identity and Intergroup Relations*. Cambridge: Cambridge University Press.

Tajfel, H., & Turner, J. (1979). An integrative theory of intergroup conflict. In H. Tajfel (Ed.), *Differentiation Between Social Groups: Studies in the Social Psychology of Intergroup Relations* (pp. 33–47). London: European Association of Experimental Social Psychology by Academic Press.

—— (1986). The social identity theory of intergroup behavior. In S. Worchel & W. Austi (Eds), *Psychology of Intergroup Relations*. Chicago: Nelson-Hall.

Tay, D. (2011). THERAPY IS A JOURNEY as a discourse metaphor. *Discourse Studies, 13*(1), 445–63.

Terkourafi, M. (2008). Toward a unified theory of politeness, impoliteness, and rudeness. In D. Bousfield & M. Locher (Eds), *Language, Power, and Social Process* (pp. 45–74). Berlin: Mouton de Gruyter.

Thelen, E., & Smith, L. B. (1994). *A Dynamic Systems Approach to the Development of Cognition and Action*. Cambridge, MA: MIT Press.

Tokunaga, M. (1992). Dichotomy in the structures of honorifics of Japanese. *Pragmatics, 2*(2), 127–40.

Turner, J. (1981). Towards a cognitive redefinition of the social group. In Henri Tajfel (Ed.), *Social Identity and Intergroup Relations* (pp. 15–40). Cambridge: Cambridge University Press.

—— (1985). Social categorization and the self-concept: A social cognitive theory of group behavior. *Advances in Group Processes: Theory and Research, 2*, 77–122.

Turner, J., & Hogg, M. (1987). *Rediscovering the Social Group*. London: Blackwell.

United States Code. Limitations on exclusive rights: Fair use, 17 USC § 107 Stat. (1976).

van Zoonen, Liesbet, Vis, Farida, & Mihelj, Sabina. (2011). YouTube interactions between agonism, antagonism and dialogue: Video responses to the anti-Islam film Fitna. *New Media & Society, 13*(8), 1283–1300.

Vis, Farida, van Zoonen, Liesbet, & Mihelj, Sabina. (2011). Women responding to the anti-Islam film Fitna: Voices and acts of citizenship on YouTube. *Feminist Review, 97*(1), 110–29.

Walther, J. B. (2002). Research ethics in Internet-enabled research: Human subjects issues and methodological myopia. *Ethics and Information Technology, 4*(3), 205–16.

Watson, D. R. (1978). Categorization, authorization and blame-negotiation in conversation. *Sociology, 12*(1), 105–13.

Wenger, E. (1998). Communities of practice: Learning as a social system. *Systems Thinker, 9*(5), 1–5.

Wenger, E., McDermott, R. A., & Snyder, W. (2002). *Cultivating Communities of Practice: A Guide to Managing Knowledge*. Cambridge, MA: Harvard Business Press.

Werkhofer, K. T. (1992). Traditional and modem views: The social constitution and the power of politeness. In R. J. Watts, S. Ide, & K. Ehlich (Eds), *Politeness in Language: Studies in Its History, Theory and Practice* (pp. 155–97). Berlin/New York: Mouton de Gruyter.

Wetherell, M. (1996). *Identities, Groups and Social Issues* (Vol. 3). London: Sage.

Wilson, Andrew. (2007). *Deluded by Dawkins? A Christian Response to the God Delusion.* Colorado Springs, CO: Kingsway Books.

Wittgenstein, L. (1953). *Philosophical Investigations.* New York: Macmillian.

Wray, M., & Newitz, A. (1997). *White Trash: Race and Class in America.* London: Routledge.

Yanow, D. (2004). Translating local knowledge at organizational peripheries. *British Journal of Management, 15*(S1), S9–S25.

YouTube. (2008). YouTube Privacy Policy. Retrieved November 11, 2008, from http://uk.youtube.com/t/privacy

Zacharias, Ravi. (2008). *The End Of Reason: A Response To The New Atheists.* Grand Rapids, MI: Zondervan.

Zadech, L. A. (1965). Fuzzy sets. *Information and Control, 8,* 338–53.

Zanotto, M. S., Cameron, L., & Cavalcanti, M. C. (Eds). (2008). *Confronting Metaphor in Use: An Applied Linguistic Approach.* Amsterdam: John Benjamins.

Key terms and concepts